THE POWER OF
PURPOSE

CREATING MEANING IN YOUR LIFE AND WORK

RICHARD J. LEIDER

MJF BOOKS

NEW YORK

Published by MJF Books
Fine Communications
Two Lincoln Square
60 West 66th Street
New York, NY 10023

The Power of Purpose
ISBN 1-56731-406-6

MJF Books and the MJF colophon are trademarks of Fine Creative Media, Inc.

10   9   8   7   6   5   4   3   2   1

For Sally, Andrew, and Greta

CONTENTS

PART III
WORKING ON PURPOSE
75

PART IV
PATHS TO PURPOSE
105

ACKNOWLEDGMENTS

Many people have helped me along my purpose path. Some have become stories in the text; for this, I offer my thanks. I also wish to thank all the wise elders, spiritual teachers, and my Inventure Group colleagues who have guided me in the matters of purpose.

I wish to express heartfelt gratitude for the vision and encouragement on this project by Steve Piersante, Pat Anderson, and their truly on-purpose team at Berrett-Koehler, who support the movement toward a more enlightened world of work. They are an author's dream team.

Dick Bolles had a huge influence on my life, career and writing and influenced my whole point of view on purpose. For this inspiration, I am eternally grateful.

And finally, love and affectionate appreciation to my wife Sally, my son Andrew, and my daughter Greta. In our relationships, I continue to discover the true power of purpose.

THE PURPOSE QUEST

Purpose.

Your aim.

Your reason for being.

Your reason for getting up in the morning.

Every one of us needs a reason to get up in the morning.

This book is about that reason. Its purpose is to help you discover the purpose for your life. Each life has a natural reason for being. Purpose is the reason a person was born. From birth to death, each of us is on a quest to discover that reason. Many never do. Yet, our world is incomplete until each one of us discovers our purpose.

Purpose is that deepest dimension within us—our central core or essence—where we have a profound sense of who we are, where we came from, and where we're going. Purpose is the quality we choose to shape our lives around. Purpose is a source of energy and direction.

Nothing shapes our lives as much as the questions we ask, or refuse to ask, throughout our lives. Purpose, however, is not a question that we can answer once and be done with it. We typically bring up the question of purpose about every ten years throughout our lives. At those times and during major life transitions, we ask questions like:

Who am I?

What am I meant to do here?

What am I trying to do with my life?

In the power of these questions lies the power of purpose. Of all the questions we might ask ourselves, these three are the most difficult to answer.

This book is for you if you're asking those three or questions such as:

- I feel that I've missed my calling in life. How do I find it?

- I've successfully reached midlife. Is that all there is? What's next?

- I've been growing spiritually. How do I connect my spiritual growth to my work?

- I'm in a major transition (divorce, job loss, retirement, graduation, death of a loved one, illness). How do I find meaning and direction?

- I have enough material success. How do I find fulfillment?

This book was developed by interviewing older adults (over age 65) about such deep questions and combining their wisdom with my studies in the fields of adult development and counseling psychology. Specifically, I asked a cross section of older adults this question: "If you could live your life over again, what would you do differently?"

Three themes wove their way through all the interviews. The older adults consistently said that if they could live their lives over again, they would:

Be more reflective.

Be more courageous.

Be clear earlier about purpose.

From these interviews, I concluded that purpose naturally resides deep inside the human soul. I observed that all people seemed to have a natural desire and capacity to contribute to life. Every one of us, somehow, wants to leave footprints. Purpose is unique to each of us, alone. Each of us is an experiment of one. We can learn from but not adopt the purpose of another. We must each discover our own.

This book builds on my earlier book *The Power of Purpose*, a paperback published by Ballantine Books in 1985, and expands and deepens the conversation. It is based on many interviews over a ten-year period with people of all ages engaged in the purpose quest. Through their input, I included many stories about people on purpose. I also included an Appendix for the many people who asked me how to use the book in their classes, book clubs, and spiritual or study groups. I chose to write this book based on my deepened personal belief that we live in a spiritual world and that every individual in that world has been created in God's image with unique gifts and a purpose to use those gifts to contribute value to the world.

Purpose is already within us. It is there waiting to be discovered. If we open ourselves up to what's inside us, we'll discover it. And once we discover it, we will have to try to live it, even if it seems totally impractical.

Purpose depends on our intuition. Intuition is that almost imperceptible voice that leads us to our purpose. Intuition is our sixth sense—the sense for the unknowable. It is independent of conscious reasoning. Sometimes we cannot explain how we know something; we just know it. To discover our purpose, we must trust our intuition.

The key to acting on purpose is to bring together the needs of the world with our unique gifts in a vocation—a calling. Calling is our way of actively contributing to our world, however we define that world. This book contains many stories of people who have acted on their calling.

Working on purpose gives us a sense of direction. Without purpose, we eventually lose our way. We live without the true joy in life and work. Until we make peace with our purpose, we will never discover fulfillment in our work or contentment with what we have.

Purpose is a way of life—a discipline to be practiced day in and day out. It requires a steady commitment to face every new workday with the question, "Why do I get up in the morning?" The wisdom to ask and the courage to answer this simple question is the essence of working on purpose.

Spirit touches and moves our lives through the mystery of purpose. That is the starting point where I begin my work of helping people discover their calling. In a pluralistic society, not everyone would agree with my starting point. That's all right. My objective, however, is not intended to express a religious or denominational belief. I do not wish to use my work as a basis for excluding people who don't believe as I do. It is, instead, the very reason for my acceptance of the many differences among people. Because of my starting point—my calling, if you will—I believe that all people have a spiritual reason for being and that our world is incomplete until each one of us discovers it.

I hope that you will discover your calling, for if I have found mine, this book will be a catalyst for finding yours.

Richard J. Leider
Minneapolis, Minnesota

PART I

THE PURPOSE OF PURPOSE

CHAPTER I

HAVE YOU MISSED YOUR CALLING?

*This is the true joy in life, the being used for a purpose recognized by
yourself as a mighty one; the being thoroughly worn out before you are
thrown on the scrap heap; the being a force of Nature instead of a feverish
selfish little clod of ailments and grievances complaining that the world will
not devote itself to making you happy.*

—GEORGE BERNARD SHAW

Inspiring words from George Bernard Shaw, but how easy it would
be to dismiss them as having no meaning for us. And yet, most of us
want to know that there is a purpose to life—that our being here
does mean something—that what we do does matter.

Most of us want to be somebody. The search to be somebody
is basic to us all. However, we often become deeply concerned about
it only when some crisis forces us to pay attention—an illness, a death,
a divorce, or a loss of job. We take life for granted until a crisis wakes
us up and forces us to ask: "Who am I?" "What am I meant to do
here?" "What am I trying to do with my life?" Crisis is the mirror of
purpose. Crisis brings us face to face with the big questions.

It's difficult to feel a clarity of purpose in the busyness of daily life. Yet, this is the first step. We must ask ourselves, "What is my busyness all about?"

One of the chief requisites for feeling the true joy in life is purpose. A constant in the lives of people who experience a sense of day-to-day aliveness is the discovery of their purpose. We need at our very core to be somebody. We need evidence to believe that we are good people and are growing or becoming as much as we can be. Clarifying our purpose helps us satisfy a basic need that we're being used for a purpose recognized by ourselves as a mighty one.

Rollie Larson, a 75-year-old retired psychologist, embodies George Bernard Shaw's "true joy in life." He lives as a whole person, integrated in mind, body, and spirit, with the natural curiosity and enthusiasm for life usually reserved for a child.

Rollie claims, "I've discovered my purpose without even thinking about it; it was a natural evolution. My purpose is 'to find my own path and help others find their path.' " This purpose gives Rollie true joy. It gives him a reason to get up in the morning. He says, "Helping others find their path has become a big thing for me. It gives me a spiritual connection in working with other people—sharing, caring, listening, loving. Part of my prayers each night are that I can make a difference in someone's life tomorrow." Rollie states, "Purpose, for me, boils down to relationships. What goes on with me and other people, that's what gives joy to me. I tried seventeen different jobs before I found that my calling was working with people!"

Growing up during World War II, Rollie's purpose was to survive, to get married someday, and to have a family. During the war his purpose was to get back into life—alive!

In the navy, Rollie's best friend told him about school counseling. "That perspective opened up a whole new world," Rollie said.

"It was like a budding flower opening up; it was a slow evolution to counseling, but it was a quick opening of the bud."

Rollie's long, esteemed counseling career took him down many paths, including founding a school counseling department, training corporate executives, opening a private practice with his wife, Doris, and writing several books. What distinguishes Rollie is his special gift and genuine capacity to listen deeply to others. His credo, "Listen to someone today," is well known to the hundreds of lives he has touched over the years. He counsels people, "If you have to go through seventeen jobs to find your calling—do it! Start opening some other windows in your areas of interest. Ultimately, your work must be a turn on; it must feel passionate."

Rollie has blended the spirit and curiosity of the child with the maturity and wisdom of age. He has discovered his purpose.

For David Shapiro, the process of discovering his purpose has been, and continues to be, an ongoing adventure from a somewhat desperate attempt to try to become someone else to a far more natural and effortless expression of who he really is.

For the first 30 years or so of his life, he struggled to adopt what he imagined to be the personal purpose of certain authors he admired, such as Woody Allen, F. Scott Fitzgerald, and others. And although this strategy made for some interesting (as well as embarrassing) moments, it was fraught with a number of problems.

David states, "I was always one step removed from myself. I was forever checking myself against an ideal (and moreover one that I had fabricated) to make life decisions that, had I been more in touch with my own calling, would have been a more authentic expression of my real self. Woody didn't finish college; neither would I. Scott went to Paris and got depressed in cafes; me too."

The whole thing was a setup that David could never win. There was no way to stack up to his heroes. No way he could ever hope to be as good at being them as they were. He could never really fully express his purpose because it wasn't his.

At some magic point, however, a change in David began taking place by almost imperceptible degrees. He says, "I found I was no longer checking the biographical notes on the blurbs of books to find out if their writers were younger or older than me when they were written. I even stopped worrying about whether my outfit was something that might be worn by one of those people whose purpose I was trying to put on, as well."

The effect of David's purpose quest, though not extremely dramatic in terms of his actual day-to-day activities, has been dramatically liberating—and radically empowering. In David's terms, "I'm no longer trying to attain someone else's purpose; I'm simply trying to express my own."

David's purpose today is captured in this statement: "Helping people to communicate with themselves and others as honestly and courageously as possible." And David is discovering his calling through his teaching and writing (my co-author!) of such works as the best-selling *Repacking Your Bags: Lighten Your Load for the Rest of Your Life*. His purpose is a beacon that lights his way. But these days, it's no longer a beacon in the distance. As he sums it up, "The light now comes from within."

Andrew Greeley, quoted in Phillip Berman's book *The Courage of Conviction*, said:

> It seems to me that in the last analysis there are only two choices: MacBeth's contention that life is a tale told by an idiot, full of sound and fury and signifying nothing, and Pierre Teilhard's "something is afoot in the universe, something that looks like gestation and birth." Either there is a plan and purpose—and that plan and purpose can best be expressed by the words "life" and "love"—or we live in a

cruel, arbitrary, and deceptive cosmos in which our lives are a brief transition between two oblivions.

Purpose is the quality we want to center our work around—the way we orient ourselves toward life and work. It is the way we make sense or meaning out of our lives. People like Rollie Larson and David Shapiro choose to center their lives around the assumption that "something is afoot in the universe, something that looks like gestation and birth."

Purpose is the recognition of the presence of the sacred within us and the choice of work that is consistent with that presence. Purpose defines our contribution to life. It may find expression through family, community, relationship, work, and spiritual activities. We receive from life what we give, and in the process we understand more of what it means to discover our purpose.

Look ahead. How old do you think you'll live to be? Imagine you're that age. As you look back on your life, what would you like to be able to say is your legacy—how you became the somebody you were destined to be? What might you do with your remaining time so that you can look back over your life with no regrets?

CHAPTER 2

LET LIFE QUESTION YOU

When we speak to our children about our own lives,
we tend to reshape our pasts to give them an illusory look of purpose.
But our children are unlikely to be able to define their goals and
then live happily ever after. Instead, they will need to reinvent themselves
again and again in response to a changing environment.

—MARY CATHERINE BATESON

Viktor Frankl suggests "Let life question you!" An openness to being questioned by life is a way to discover our purpose, to find out who we are. Frankl suggests that many of us are questioning life, rather than letting it question us. We ask: What has life done for me? Will things go my way today? What's in it for me? Many of us question life in this way. However, there is a more profound wisdom in reversing the questioning and letting life question us.

It is often in the midst of a crisis that we pull back from the entanglements of daily survival and let life question us. The benefit of a crisis is often the letting go of petty concerns, conflicts, and the need for control and the realization that life is short and every moment precious. But why wait for a crisis?

Cancer therapists Carl and Stephanie Simonton give their patients this advice:

> You must stop and reassess your priorities and values. You
> must be willing to be yourself, not what people want you to
> be because you think that is the only way you can get love.
> You can no longer be dishonest. You are now at a point
> where, if you truly want to live, you have to be who you are.

Could there be any better advice for us?

Whenever we are confronted with a crisis, like cancer or a fate that is unavoidable, then we are given a choice to express our highest calling, to fulfill our deepest purpose. What matters is the attitude we take toward the crisis.

A sense of purpose is rarely handed to us. We get it by deciding to have it. We get it by deciding that, yes, I matter. A sense of purpose comes from within, and only we know if we have it. Only we know if there is something in our life that makes us want to get up in the morning.

One purpose in life is not more important than another. There is purpose whenever we use our gifts and talents to respond to something we believe in.

Terry Fox is a clear example. For this young Canadian, the necessity to discover his purpose was thrust upon him early in life. Two days after his eighteenth birthday, Terry learned he had a cancerous tumor in his right knee. His leg would have to be amputated immediately, since the cancer could spread through the rest of his body. Now, suddenly, life was tentative, no longer to be taken for granted. Despite the shock and the speed with which Terry's life had changed, he spent little time in the trap of self-pity. Within the confines of his hospital room, Terry detected a purpose, his personal reason to live.

Many of us will be forced to reflect upon the reason for our existence when we experience severe crises. But, as Terry Fox put it: "you don't have to do like I did—wait until you lose a leg or get some awful disease—before you can take the time to find out what kind of stuff you're made of. Start now. Anybody can."

Two weeks after his surgery, Terry began chemotherapy. The cancer clinic and the painful treatments were a reminder to Terry that almost half of all cancer patients never recover. Terry could no longer take his life for granted. He decided he wanted to do something for the people who were still there. He began to detect what it was he cared deeply about; what moved him. Terry began to discover a new sense of purpose.

He would run all the way across Canada to raise one million dollars to fight cancer. He would give the money to the Canadian Cancer Society.

After running three-fifths of the way across Canada, Terry Fox had to leave his Marathon of Hope. The power of purpose had transformed an average athlete into a person who, with an artificial leg, ran a marathon a day for five months! He never finished. The cancer had spread to his lungs.

By the time of his death, one year later, he had raised many millions of dollars and had inspired hundreds of thousands of people.

Terry Fox had a direct impact on my own life. I saw him "on purpose" in Ontario. While camping around the perimeter of Lake Superior, I came upon Terry Fox running just outside of Thunder Bay. Sandwiched in between the flashing red lights of a highway patrol car and the van with a "Marathon of Hope" banner on its side was Terry Fox—with a look in his eyes that is etched indelibly in my mind. That look of determination was the power of purpose in action. That unexpected meeting planted the seed that led to the writing of this book.

He challenged me with that look. He made me ask, "What am I trying to do with my life?"

Ever since I was a child, I've had an intense curiosity about what motivates people. I've always felt convinced that there could be more to my life if only I could find it. Tempted by the glowing promises of self-help books, I read them all, and they all said, "The first step is to decide what your goals in life are." So I sat down cheerfully one day with pencil in hand to jot down my goals. They didn't come!

The self-help books had suggested that I should want some definite goals (e.g., to be successful, to earn so much money). But none of these goals moved me. I was unable to find that clear passion like Terry Fox had, that would make my goals meaningful. I was beginning to question whether there might not be something wrong with me.

Whenever I did manage to commit myself to a goal, I found I achieved more success than I ever expected, but the results never brought me the fulfillment promised by the books. I had never been able to find, in one of those goals, a meaningful focus for my life. On one day, a certain goal would be important; on another day, a different goal would capture my fancy. I rarely committed myself to anything passionately. I wanted to work for a cause, not just for a living.

Terry Fox got me thinking again. I started to realize that I needed to embrace a purpose by which I could deliberately guide my work life—a purpose that went beyond just earning a living. I began to shape a new vision for my work; not the shaping of work to fit my ego-driven goals, but the gradual detecting of a purpose outside of myself.

Terry Fox symbolized what most of us want to know—that there is purpose to life, that our being here does mean something, that what we do does matter. The sheer determination of one individual can turn a seemingly mediocre idea into a clear success. Behind the creation of any great deed is at least one individual who was consumed by a purpose to make a difference. The only place we can find this kind of motivation is within.

In describing people like Terry Fox who have discovered a sense of purpose, I once felt a certain uneasiness. I didn't want to be describing an unrealistic goal-oriented ideal. Purpose had always meant goals to me.

Terry Fox changed all that. He evidenced the true joy I sought for my own life. He was alive! It is not what goals we have that give us aliveness, it is the sense of purpose with which we embrace them. People with a sense of purpose learn to move the focus of their attention and concern away from themselves to others. They have learned to let life question them.

CHAPTER 3

THE ESSENCE OF PURPOSE

God made man because He loved stories.

—ISAK DINESEN

Life begins with questions. Nothing shapes our lives as much as the questions we ask—or refuse to ask—throughout our lives. On the first day of each new year, and about every ten years, my gaze turns inward toward fresh questions. Eventually, however, I seem to arrive back at the beginning with the age-old questions—the toughest, yet essential ones: "Who am I?" "What am I meant to do here?" "What am I trying to do with my life?"

If God loves stories, as Isak Dinesen suggests, what's your story? How do you answer those three essential questions? The differences in the quality of our lives often lies in the quality of the questions that shape our stories. And without each of our stories, the story of the universe would be incomplete.

Mary Foley's story was ended before she was able to complete it. Mary believed deeply in human potential, and she believed in herself. Her calling was "To be a positive influence on the lives of women and children." Mentoring other women in her field was the work she loved. Believing in the dreams of other young professional women, Mary discovered her gifts, discovered her passions, and shared her own struggles and questions.

Mary frequently checked on what people were reading, talked about what she was reading, and often recommended or gave books to others. She discovered an earlier version of this book and gave it to many people. She inquired and was genuinely interested in people's questions, especially around purpose.

As corporate manager of health services for a major manufacturing company, Mary was one of those rare mentors who consistently held high expectations of people and encouraged them not to settle for less than their higher purpose. Following a mentoring theme of "just do it!", she was always the one to go up against any challenge. She never gave up on people's potential.

Mary was tragically murdered. As a community, we lost in a huge way when Mary's creative light was tragically snuffed out. We lost in terms of her unselfishness and love for other people. Giving her gifts benefited the entire community, not only through the direct contributions she made to mentoring others but through the living example she provided of the essence of purpose.

To understand the essence of purpose adequately, we must look to a deeper underlying belief. It is an old belief but an enduring one that is reexamined in every era. The nature of this belief is summed up well by the historian Arnold Toynbee in his *Study of History* (Vol. III):

> These religious founders [Jesus, Buddha, Lao Tse, Saint Francis of Assisi] disagreed with each other in their pictures of
> what is the nature of the universe, the nature of spiritual life,
> the nature of ultimate spiritual reality. But they all agreed in

their ethical precepts. They all agreed that the pursuit of
material wealth is a wrong aim. . . . They all spoke in favor of
unselfishness and of love for other people as the key to happiness and to success in human affairs.

Most religions and spiritual traditions speak of an essence at
the center of ourselves. It is what most call God and some call the
Higher Power, the Soul, the Divine, the Sacred, the Spirit, or the
Essence, and it represents who we are at the core. People who live
and work on purpose know how to express this essence consistently.

Mary helped many young women express their essence. She
played her role in creating the kind of world she dreamed of. An
organization called The Friends of Mary Foley keeps her essence
active in the community. Every year since her tragic death over ten
years ago, a group of her friends get together on her birthday to celebrate and toast her life. Each year they raise money and resources
for a cause that aligns with Mary's purpose. One of her friends said,
"She lived with more purpose than most anyone I have known."

Mary's sister, Kathy, said, "I raised my children differently and
I live for the day. I learned from Mary how to genuinely support my
kids to be creative, to try things they normally wouldn't. Every single day, my memories of Mary come up and I stop and look at people as they are, instead of as they're supposed to be. Mary's death
opened my eyes to life." If Mary's death opened your eyes to life,
then her purpose remains alive in this book. We never know the rip-
ples that our lives might cause years after our actions.

Every one of us eventually faces our own story, the time when
we are challenged to define our life on this planet, our reason for
being here. Our story often surfaces with a crisis or transition in life
when our standard answers to the big questions no longer satisfy us.

The question, "What is my story?" interests many of us as we
age. There is an emerging group of "discoverers" who are living in

the big questions. Many of my friends, colleagues, and clients, who several years ago would have been embarrassed to discuss their stories, are now talking openly about spiritual journeys, meaningful work, and fulfilling relationships. Personally, my answer to the question is still evolving and deepening after many years of shaping it. My own life has been a history of questioning, discovering, and integrating more elements of my self into my work. On my way to becoming a school psychologist, I became a corporate career coach.

In my early twenties, I was a counseling psychology graduate student with the military draft board hounding me to complete my studies and begin my compulsory military service. In an effort to find a solution I could live with, I joined an army psychological operations reserve unit. That choice required me to leave my schooling in Colorado with my master of arts and return to Minnesota. Along with the move came the necessity of supporting my family. During my job hunting process, I accidentally discovered the corporate human resources field. Joining a large Fortune 100 company, I worked under a great mentor in a variety of human resource positions, ending up, after two years, as training manager. In my training role, I had the opportunity to coach a large number of employees who were unclear about their career direction.

I knew, from my counseling psychology training, that there were many effective ways of helping people clarify their career direction. In the late 1960s, however, there were few practical books or programs available. So, I started creating my own ideas, exercises, and programs and trying them out after hours. Soon I had a burgeoning career coaching practice after hours, a growing reputation, and a waiting list!

With a growing family and financial needs, I moved to a large bank holding company, where, in addition to a much larger human resources job, I continued to hone my career coaching skills both inside the organization and after hours. I was, however, still a lone voice in the career wilderness.

A chance meeting with Richard Bolles, author of the classic book *What Color Is Your Parachute?*, fueled my career coaching fires and affirmed my evolving coaching philosophy. Dick gave me the opportunity to preview what was later to become his 25-year best-selling book. From Dick, a former Episcopalian priest, I got support for my intuitive feeling that every individual has been created in God's image with true gifts and worth. Dick helped me clarify a belief for which I am eternally grateful: "The gifts of each of us and the value of serving others provide our mission in life." Dick sparked my interest in studying about purpose—a passion that has guided much of my work and remains with me to this day.

In addition to Dick Bolles, a chance meeting with Sigurd Olson also fueled my passion about purpose. I wanted to write about purpose. As a budding writer, I had heroes and models I wanted to imitate, and Sigurd Olson was one of them.

Sigurd was a wilderness philosopher and ardent conservationist who wrote about nature and spirituality. He focused on the purpose connection that we feel when we're in the presence of nature. I was deeply moved by his writing. His books found their way into both my backpack and my briefcase.

I corresponded with him over several years, and he encouraged my purpose and my writing. In an essay on his own writing in his book *Open Horizons*, he wrote: "Occasionally, when I did no writing at all, my spirits fell and everything seemed without meaning or purpose." The cure, he advised, was to begin again. When he began writing again, his spirit soared. He said that he wrote about things as he saw them and the passion just came through. When I was down or blocked in my writing, Sigurd inspired me to begin again, to follow my passion.

During this same time period, I applied for and received a Bush Foundation Fellowship to study mid-career issues. I designed my own nondegree customized fellowship (there were few programs available at the time) under the umbrella of the Harvard Business School. Through my fellowship studies, I discovered the need for and value of career coaching in organizational settings.

When I returned, I quickly moved into full-time career coaching work. I studied it intensely and seemed to have a natural gift for it. I launched a successful one-to-one coaching practice. From that start I moved to leading workshops, co-writing my first book, speaking to groups, and guiding wilderness renewal retreats.

Helping others discover their purpose became my purpose. It chose me. I discovered my purpose on the way to somewhere else. Today my purpose is "to help people discover their purpose and express their calling while they're still alive." It moves me. It gets me up in the morning excited to go to work. And it fulfills my need to connect deeply with people's lives—to add real value.

As a graduate student in counseling psychology, I used to regularly ask my professors, "What is the purpose of life?" Carl Rogers, the founder of client-centered Rogerian psychology, helped answer that question for me. His model of human behavior was based on a concept he called "congruence." To fulfill our purpose as human beings, he determined, we needed to be congruent between three levels. The core level, our essence, needs to be congruent with our middle level, which is what we perceive ourselves to be. And the surface level, our form, which is the actual behaviors we show to others, needs to match how it is inside us.

Congruence, according to Rogers, means living from the inside out. It means "turning ourselves inside out"—being aware of our essence and living it. His theory changed my life.

Before, during, and since graduate school I have had a passion for listening to people tell their stories. In fact, the passion extends back into my early childhood. With a lifelong love of people's stories, my purpose has naturally evolved to seeing and helping others see the theme—the purpose—of their own life stories. As I have had the profound privilege to listen to hundreds of people's stories over the last decade, my point of view on purpose has evolved. This book is grounded in my beliefs, my own story, and other people's stories. It represents my present understanding of what I have learned about purpose. Here are my present beliefs about purpose and the thinking from which they come. To discover your purpose, you must:

- Discover how to live from the inside out

- Discover your gifts

- Discover what moves you

- Discover solitude

DISCOVER HOW TO LIVE FROM THE INSIDE OUT

I have written this book as one who is constantly working to find my purpose. I taught myself, and became aware through wise teachers and elders, that we are all born with a purpose. We live in a purposeful universe. Every organism in the universe has a design—a purpose that determines its function and role. A critical part of our development is the inside-out search for purpose and meaning. The true lesson in life is to turn ourselves inside out to discover that our purpose already exists within.

Each life has a natural built-in reason for being. That reason is to make a positive contribution to the world around it. Purpose is the creative positive spirit of life moving through us, from the inside out. It is the deep, mysterious dimension in each of us—our essence—where we have a profound intuitive sense of who we are, where we came from, and where we are going.

Each of us must have a purpose built into our essence. Otherwise, we would not, in our deepest moments, ask: "Who am I?" "What am I meant to do here?" "What am I trying to do with my life?" Our life quest is shaped by the inside-out questions we ask, or fail to ask, during our deepest moments.

DISCOVER YOUR GIFTS

Purpose helps us create a larger meaning for our lives. It feeds our three deep spiritual hungers:

- to connect deeply with the creative spirit of life

- to actively know and express our gifts

- to know our lives have made a difference.

Our talents are gifts of spirit to us, but we must discover them and choose the calling in which we invest them. When we work on purpose, we bring together the needs of the world—what moves us—with our special gifts in a vocation, or calling.

DISCOVER WHAT MOVES YOU

Purpose is the conscious choice of what, where, and how to make a positive contribution to our world. It is the theme, quality, or passion we choose to center our lives around. Once we discover our gifts and what moves us, the whole world takes on a new energy. Our life becomes a thing of spiritual significance.

Our world is incomplete until each one of us discovers what moves us—our passion. No other person can hear our calling. We must listen and act on it for ourselves. To hear it, we need a positive environment that supports deep listening and truth telling.

DISCOVER SOLITUDE

In the power of our questions lies the power of purpose. To hear our calling, we need a regular practice of solitude to listen to our deepest yearnings. The purpose quest requires the wisdom of periodic quiet and contemplation.

There are no shortcuts to purpose. Within each of us lies the capacity to slow down, to detect our calling. Too few of us these days seem to be enjoying the journey. Instead, many of us have become climbers, scrambling up and over rocky boulders, out of breath, each hoping to reach a plateau where there will be time to enjoy the view. Many of us yearn to stop and savor the climb and feel more joy along the way.

Mountains have always drawn us toward them, wherever they are. Mountains are metaphors for our own stories. René Daumal captured the essence of purpose in *Mount Analogue:*

> In the mythic tradition the Mountain is the bond between
> Earth and Sky. Its solitary summit reaches the sphere of eternity, and its base spreads out in manifold foothills into the
> world of mortals. It is the way by which man can raise himself
> to the divine and by which the divine can reveal itself to man.

Many of us discover our purpose by renewing our connection with the divine in nature. We go to the mountain for an experience of solitude. When we step into nature or onto a mountain, there is an eternal mystery that questions us: "Who are you?" "What are you here to do?" "What are you trying to do with your life?"

Purpose is not merely a concept; it is a practice. Until we make peace with our purpose, we will never discover true joy in our work or contentment with what we have.

Use the following guideline to discover purpose in your life: "My purpose in life is to discover my gifts; to discover what moves me; and to actively bring my gifts and passions together in the world." Take a pencil and paper and write an initial draft purpose statement: "My purpose in life is . . .". Then in a sentence or two try to state clearly what you feel your present purpose is or might be.

If finding your calling seems beyond reach now, take a segment of it, a day, for example, and put it in writing: "My purpose for the next day of my life is . . .".

Take your time, but keep at it until you have a purpose that moves you, for the time being at least. We will continue to look at the essence of purpose—the four beliefs—throughout the book.

CHAPTER 4

A DEEPER CALL

In our time, we workers are being called to reexamine our work:
how we do it; whom it is helping or hurting; what it is we do;
and what we might be doing if we were to let go of our
present work and follow a deeper call.

—MATTHEW FOX

If we are being called, who is doing the calling? I meet many people today who are letting go of their work to find new work. They feel called.

A deeper call comes from the inside out; it is the expression of our essence, our core. Our calling is an expression of the spirit at work in the world through us. It is that mysterious voice that calls us to give our gifts.

To follow a deeper call, we must understand that purpose is an inside-out process for:

- Organizing our lives.

- Providing meaning.

- Following our heart.

- Clarifying our calling.

Purpose is our deepest dimension—our essence—where we have a profound sense of who we are, where we came from, and where we are going.

Purpose is not a thing. It's never a static condition we can preserve. Purpose is a continuous activity, questions we ask over and over again. It's a process we live every day. It's a process for listening and shaping our life stories.

It's tempting to ignore the question of purpose in life, since the consequences of our neglect usually don't show up until crisis points or toward the very end of our lives. Thus, we unconsciously spend much of our energy staying busy, building a lifestyle and making a living.

Yet, when we scratch under the surface of our drive for making a living, what's there?

If we strive for success as an end in itself, we never find it. Affluent society has given many of us the means to success, but often we still cannot see the true joy, a purpose to live for.

Commitment to something larger than our own success gives life meaning. To what are we committed? What are we going to do with our success once we get it?

The power of purpose is a process for discovering our calling. This appropriate relationship with the work world is what Buddhists call "right livelihood" and what Christians call "stewardship."

Dr. Albert Schweitzer called this notion "reverence for life." Late one afternoon in September, 1915, Dr. Schweitzer was sitting on the deck of a small steamboat making its way up the Ogooue River to Lambarene in Central Africa. He was bringing medical services to the local population in French Equatorial Africa. The boat was moving cautiously through a herd of hippopotamuses in the river. As Schweitzer watched the ship's captain maneuver to avoid hitting the animals, he came to a profound realization—the captain represented the highest purpose: reverence for the life of other creatures. For years Schweitzer had been searching for the key ethic in the modern world. He found it in Africa—"reverence for life."

Schweitzer recognized that far more people are idealistic than will admit to being so. He stated:

> Just as the water of the streams we see is small in amount compared to that which flows underground, so the idealism which becomes visible in small amount compared with what men and women bear locked in their hearts, unreleased or scarcely released. To unbind what is bound, to bring the underground waters to the surface: mankind is waiting and longing for such as can do that.

It's an odd quirk that makes us suppress our idealism. Opportunities for following a deeper call are virtually everywhere. To follow a deeper call, we must understand that purpose can help us organize our lives, provide meaning, follow our heart, and clarify our calling.

ORGANIZING OUR LIVES

Many of us are starved for coherence in our lives. Purpose can serve as a coherent focus for our time, talent, and money. The most effective people know how to carry out daily activities while keeping their eye on a longer-range vision and purpose they want to center their lives around.

Purpose has a way of ordering time and energies around itself; that is the real power behind the purpose! It often involves refocusing our work in order to bring out our talents and full potential.

When we are moved by something, many things previously felt to be important fade in significance. If our purpose is genuine enough, it involves us deeply and orders all areas of our life. We begin to eliminate what is irrelevant and what is so much clutter. A simplification takes place, and we achieve a clarity as to what we're about. We don't need to pretend to be what we're not. What is of real importance stands out more clearly.

In his seminal book *Voluntary Simplicity*, Duane Elgin quoted these remarks from Richard Gregg, who coined the term *voluntary simplicity*:

> Voluntary simplicity involves both inner and outer condition. It
> means singleness of purpose, sincerity and honesty within, as well
> as avoidance of exterior clutter, of many possessions irrelevant to
> the chief purpose of life. It means an ordering and guiding of
> our energy and our desires, a partial restraint in some directions
> in order to secure greater abundance of life in other directions. It
> involves a deliberate organization of life for a purpose.

Richard Peterson has been moving toward simplicity for over twenty years. As the former president of Vail Associates and, later, Durango Ski Corporation, Richard's mission was to bring joy to others. And, in the process, Richard has been rediscovering the joy in his own life. Today, he lives a simple yet varied life, with many aspects, including part-time chief financial officer of a small but growing company, a part-time financial coaching practice, and member of several nonprofit boards of directors.

During his executive tenure, he rarely had time for listening to a deeper call; his life was filled with "doing," not listening. When he left the executive ranks, it still did not solve his "doingness" problem. He says, "My biggest challenge was simplifying and being fully present for life. Discovering my calling was not something that jumped out at me."

Richard relates, "The natural world is my spiritual teacher. It started when I started backpacking in the form of a connection with something bigger than me. I observed, through nature, that we're all connected in one big web. The web includes all life, like dogs, gardens, and people."

Richard's purpose today is "To nurture my own and others' spiritual growth; to demonstrate love and gratitude for all that I am by doing something everyday that expresses love to a fellow human, animal, or plant; and to balance interaction with nature with helping others develop a healthy relationship with money and prosperity."

The way to spend our precious time and energy wisely is to know the purpose for which we live and then to deliberately organize our lives accordingly.

PROVIDING MEANING

Following a deeper call in our lives means that something (an aim, a passion, an interest, a problem, an idea) attracts us enough to move us to action on its behalf and is important enough so that focusing on it directs our activities and provides our lives with a sense of meaning.

Benjamin Jackson was running in a local 10K weekend race where there were a number of wheelchair athletes. Post-race conversation led Ben to an awareness of the challenges these athletes faced in their normal day-to-day activities. Soon he explored the realities of wheelchair life at the college he was attending and at his mother's workplace. He began writing letters and lobbying his school's administration to provide funds for greater accessibility for students with disabilities. Ben went on to study architecture and now consults with organizations on making their buildings more accessible to people with physical challenges. Fulfilling work began with a 10K race and today serves as Ben's calling.

Purpose helps us understand what is relevant to life, what it is we live for, who we are, and what we are about in actual day-to-day living. Our world makes sense to us. Living a meaningful life means living in the deep questions of life. We are steadied and whole in our living, and the various situations of day-to-day living are more easily handled. Such a unifying sense of direction can withstand much stress and is actually strengthened by overcoming difficulties.

Through purpose, we are more responsive to ourselves, just as artists are more in touch with themselves when absorbed in the creation of a painting. There is a selflessness that goes with being absorbed in something we genuinely find interesting; yet it is a sense of being more ourselves.

We are born purpose-seeking creatures. Purpose is necessary for our very health and survival. If you doubt this, check out the rates of illness and death when people lose or give up their sense of purpose. People who retire without something to retire to have a much higher incidence of mortality and illness than do those who have a focus.

Why is this? Is it natural aging? I think not. Work provides an ongoing sense of meaning—a positive reason for getting up in the morning. And, as if by magic, life returns the favor by being fuller, richer, and more meaningful.

At a U.S. university, when 60 students were asked why they had attempted suicide, 85% said the reason had been that "life seemed meaningless." More important, however, was that 93% of these students suffering from the apparent lack of purpose in their lives were socially active, achieving academically, and on good terms with their families. As Viktor Frankl pointed out:

> This happens in the midst of affluent societies and in the
> midst of welfare states! For too long we have been dreaming a

dream from which we are now waking up: the dream that if you just improve the socio-economic status of people, everything will be OK, people will become happy. The truth is that as the struggle for survival has subsided, the question has emerged: survival for what? Ever more people today have the means to live, but no meaning to live for.

We cannot have deep and enduring satisfaction unless we have self-worth. We cannot have self-worth unless our lives are an earnest attempt to express the finest and most enduring qualities that we are aware of. Purpose is an important condition for an enduring satisfaction with life.

Through following a deeper call, we discover and create the meaning of our lives. And in acting on our purpose, we live the meaning of our lives. We realize the point of our lives, what direction we are to go.

FOLLOWING OUR HEART

If purpose is important enough to give direction and meaning to our lives, it must also align with our hearts. We must be able to make use of our special gifts. Through following a deeper call, we come to a truer appreciation of our strengths, as well as our limitations, and we can take pride in the successful use of our strengths.

Purpose enables us to be complete, just as painting enables artists to complete parts of themselves. Through our gifts, purpose is activated in our lives rather than merely professed. Purpose is not ready-made; it must be shaped and clarified through our acting on it.

Purpose means using our gifts on what deeply moves us. Occupying ourselves and our time with people, commitments, and challenges that help us feel worthwhile means giving our gifts to someone or something we believe in.

Susan Boren stopped one day, in the midst of her hectic life as a retail corporation executive, to consider how much of her time was going into work. Like many of us, she quickly discovered that it added up to most of her life. She figured out that she was trading too much of her life doing work she did not enjoy to get the personal creative time she desperately wanted. She began a quest to find a way to put her heart and soul back into her work. The time had come for new answers as her journey turned inward. Susan states, "For me now, there's a drumbeat inside in anticipation of the dance. My new energy for work needs an outlet, a place to dance!"

The process of making a major work change is disruptive. Following a deeper call puts significant strains on our relationships. Susan puts it this way: "I've made hard choices to move away from people who don't share my values and to seek people who understand where I'm coming from."

With major change, we often confront, as seldom before, our own insecurities and self-doubts as we let go of the identity of the past and risk shaping our future. Susan relates, "In my past life, you could get into trouble for speaking your truth. Now, I feel I'm in trouble if I don't speak it! That's been the most freeing element in the last year. Speaking the truth creates so much energy."

Susan is discovering the work she loves and has begun taking positive steps to realize it. She says, "I'm not going to discover a new medicine or build a new rocket, but, somehow, I can move people to work differently with each other. My purpose now is to be in the world every day on purpose, in relationships, in work and in nature in ways that are true to who I am . . . and ways that express my gifts of perception, synthesis, and leadership, creating growth in myself, others and organizations."

We cannot force a particular purpose to be more important than it is, just as we cannot force ourselves to be genuinely passionate about someone or something. The way to know the true depth of some purpose is to begin it! Through giving our gifts, we help to both create purpose and to discover it.

Many years ago a close friend, Rolf, asked me, "Are you enjoying your work?" He had been reading the Tao Te Ching, which states, "In work, do what you enjoy." Actually, I had been asking myself that same question—but conveniently either not listening or denying my own response.

In answering my friend, I said, "Things are okay. I believe what I'm doing is making a contribution—you know—doing something worthwhile. But no, I don't feel like I'm really enjoying my work. In fact, I feel as though I'm waiting for something to happen—for something to move me one way or another!"

The speed of my response surprised me. Actually, I had never considered work as joy. Work was work. I began reflecting on my friend's question. It gradually became clear to me that even if I was doing a worthwhile thing, if I was not enjoying it, something was wrong. Perhaps it was not the best use of my gifts.

Wanting to understand why I seemed to be feeling more struggle than joy, I began to see my false belief—that "work is work and not to be enjoyed." Confronting that belief, by which I had been living my life, led to a whole cascade of insights about the role of work in my life.

As I began acting on these insights, prompted by the question of a friend and found through further reflection, I chose to make a radical change in my work life. My new belief became, "We have a natural hunger for and deep need for joy in our work!"

Activities that derive from a deeper call are not a burden forced on us. Through purpose, we grow by becoming more honest with ourselves and more aware of our gifts that naturally give us joy.

Honesty is present in realizing that my particular gifts are not in any way superior. What is really important is not whether my gifts are more important than your gifts but that we each have important gifts to share with the world.

Genuine purpose means overcoming the arrogance that exaggerates my own gifts at the expense of yours. I am able to present myself as I am without self-display; I don't need to pretend to be what I am not. There is nothing for others to see through. My purpose rings true. There is not a significant gap between how I act and what I really feel. I hear a deeper call.

CLARIFYING OUR CALLING

Are you bored with work? Do you lack day-to-day energy and vitality? These conditions often occur because we don't have work aligned with our talents and passions. Often it's because our work doesn't move us.

Many organizations and many countries, like many individuals, seem to be in a period of purpose drift. They appear to have lost a sense of vision and direction. Many people seem to be waiting for a leader or a significant event to call forth a new vision. The uncertainty and growing restlessness have prompted a new willingness to think the unthinkable, to seriously consider what life means and where we wish to go. There is reason to think that the kind of power fostered by a sense of purpose is especially appropriate in our times and circumstances.

A sense of purpose urgency seems to be dictated by our many serious societal problems. The prospects of growing terrorist activities worldwide, the growing demands of many nations for a more equitable share of the world's resources, the prospect that we may poison ourselves to death with environmental pollutants, a growing voter apathy, the chronic fiscal crises in many of our largest cities, the shift from an industrial to an information economy, and the challenge to the legitimacy of leaders in nearly all major institutions drive the purpose quest. These are but a few of the many issues that make the rediscovery of purpose an appropriate response to a pressing situation. Our needs as individuals uniquely match the needs of our organizations, our society, and our planet.

The activist cares for this cause, the writer cares for that idea, the parent cares for this child, the leader cares for that organization, and so on. Purpose means each of us following a deeper call. It means living inside the question, "Am I making a living doing the work I love to do?" It means being able to say, "Does my life matter?"

Each of us following a deeper calling is the key to survival in the 21st century. It's easy to say that we value a clean environment; it's tougher to figure out what to do about it on a day-to-day basis. It's tougher, but more rewarding, when we back up our principles with action. There are numerous ways to get action. The trick is to find the cause that moves us and the role that fits our most unique gifts.

A deeper call consciously started for Dan Petersen when he completed his studies to become an orthodontist. Looking back, Dan says, "I was operating with an undeclared purpose to set my life up with enough money and enough time to follow my longing for adventure. I wanted to work half of the year and be adventurous with the other half."

And Dan did just that for 22 years. At that point, he left a successful private practice to follow his calling to study "holistic healing." He recalls, "Something very powerful was calling me; so powerful, I was willing to give up almost everything to discover it. It was in the form of a question—'How does self-healing occur?' "

He left his practice to return to school to study his passion—the body-mind connection. He believed that self-healing systems can function optimally when we remove the habits and hindrances to normal growth.

Dan's purpose today is "To provide environments where self-healing can occur." He has the same calling he had 15 years ago but in a new form. As a change management workshop instructor for corporations, he provides an environment where the body of a corporation can self-heal when causal issues are identified and addressed.

Dan believes that the optimal environment for human life is the same as for corporate life—"freedom of expression, meaningful purpose, compassion, and balance." His purpose continues to evolve and broaden to encompass the "health care for humanity."

Purpose clarifies our calling. It gives our work meaning. We know why we get up in the morning. Purpose serves as the glue that holds the various aspects of our work together. It gives our work greater focus and energy. It serves as an inner guide by which we can judge appropriate responses to events, people, places, and time.

Purpose is the passion that shapes our work life. When we commit ourselves to the idea of purpose in general, we never know when a particular situation or need is going to call us. Purpose often comes in surprises. It often comes in the form of a still, small, creative voice that is only faintly heard above the noise of a busy lifestyle.

There are many voices calling in our world that we don't hear because we are not listening—or perhaps because we don't feel capable of acting if we did listen. The world we hear tends to be the world we listen for.

There is not a community or organization that does not offer abundant opportunity for purpose to every person living there. Purpose starts with discovering what is needed and wanted and producing it right where you are!

Victor Hugo wrote, "Nothing in this world is so powerful as an idea whose time has come." Yet, it's a funny thing about people and their ideas. Most of the time the idea is the only thing they're willing to risk.

There has never been a monopoly on creative ideas; but the number of people who are moved by an idea, and who will risk taking a stand on their idea, is small indeed.

The most fortunate people on earth are those who have found a calling that's bigger than they are—that moves them and fills their lives with constant passion, aliveness, and growth—who, as Matthew Fox put it, "follow a deeper call."

PART II

LIVING ON PURPOSE

CHAPTER 5

WHY DO YOU GET UP ON MONDAY MORNING?

*Purpose is a profound commitment to a
compelling expectation for the time of your life.*

—FREDERIC HUDSON & PAMELA McLEAN

Many of us say we don't have enough time to take care of our lives and careers. Then before we know it, we're right! It's easy to get so busy living our lives that we don't have time to notice time passing.

One of the things most visible in our society is that many people are very busy doing many, many things, often with enormous intensity. If you look more closely, you realize that, in a way, we are busy trying to survive and to find recognition for our worth. We do many things in order to answer the question, "Why do you get up in the morning?" Busyness is a way of gaining approval for our self-worth. Busyness is also a status symbol. But it is a nervous way of living because we continuously seek approval from outside ourselves and then end up saying, "What am I trying to do with my life?"

Recently, many of us have come to acknowledge publicly what we privately knew all along. Namely, that by successfully surviving adolescence and early adulthood, we did not ensure ourselves of a tranquil, jolt-free passage through the rest of our lives and careers. We change; our priorities and values shift; confidence grows, dissolves into doubt, then back again; relationships evolve; careers and lifestyles become static or take on new meanings. Forming a complex life cycle, we're either growing or stagnating, building or slipping.

Recently, it occurred to psychologist Fred Kiel that he was losing his passion for his work. He was beginning, at age 56, to question why he was getting up and going to work on Monday morning. He was also questioning his stressful travel schedule. He says, "I was suddenly very hungry to see to it that all parts of my life hung together as one integrated whole."

He started the journey to wholeness when he was about 3 years old. He recalls, "I can remember as a very young child being puzzled about human nature—and perhaps most of all puzzled about my own nature and experience. I have continually sought answers in a variety of ways from my parents and authority figures. My parents were loving and well-meaning people, but they rarely talked to me about the big questions."

From parents and authority figures, Fred turned next to "the god of our modern world—science." He turned away from heart to head and spent a couple of decades searching for meaning through biology and psychology. Eventually, he tired of that struggle and concluded that "the only real security in this life was to have financial independence."

That "dry hole" didn't last as long. Financial success didn't deliver either meaning or independence.

So, for the past several years, he has been listening—listening to his clients, his friends, his wife, and his children. But most of all, he relates, "I've been listening to my heart, to quiet voices when I meditate, pray, and worship. I've been listening when I walk on our farmland. And I've been quietly led to seek wisdom and answers from the most unlikely places."

Fred became fascinated with and a student of the Amish culture. He claims that the Amish live by specific decision rules. Before they will embrace a new invention or accept a change, it must first be demonstrated to the elders that it both enhances and supports family and community life. And it must not be something that harms the earth, as the Amish see themselves as stewards of the earth.

Studying and visiting the Amish has helped Fred "peel the layers of the onion to arrive at the heart," or more precisely, at his heart! From this point forward, Fred wants to live in ways similar to the Amish values. He wants his behavior to enhance his and others' family life. He wants his behavior to enhance his and others' community life and to have a low impact on the environment.

Living with these values in mind has helped Fred reshape a lot of his choices. It's no longer enough to just get up on Monday morning to make money as a psychologist. He states, "I still want to make money, but I now want to work on purpose. I want my professional behavior to meet my values. I want to work with clients who I know are in alignment with my purpose."

Fred's purpose each Monday morning is simply this: "In all relationships I want to be a force to help people with matters of the heart." He believes that when people are grounded and live well from their hearts, they naturally tend to make choices that are good for family life, for community life, and for the environment.

Like the Amish, Fred has a spiritual basis to his personal calling. As he sums it up, "I want to devote the balance of my life to serving God as I have come to understand the divine." Fifty-six years along the purpose journey, he feels at peace about many of the mysteries of life. He's concluded, "I don't need to understand any more about human nature than I already know, and I guess I don't understand it much more than I did at age 3."

Every one of us, simply because we are human, periodically wonders, "What am I here to do?" Most spiritual traditions—Buddhism, Hinduism, Judaism, Christianity, and Islam—deal with this question. We have to work at finding our true self. If we act on a false self, the self that is put together by a mask of approval and busyness, we will always jump from one illusion to another. We will never be deeply satisfied.

We need to start unmasking our illusions. Slowly, we need to discover what part of busyness is just cultural consensus (i.e., norms we accept) and what part is an expression of our real purpose.

We're often unaware of why we're uneasy or discontent. We're like train passengers who don't know where the train is now or where it's going. Often we're surprised at where it travels and where it stops, but we stay on for the ride. Achieving a clearer purpose for our lives often requires that we reroute ourselves—change our direction or destination or prepare ourselves for unexpected stops and detours. We don't have to be locked onto one track if we don't want to be; there are switches we can throw all through life.

For every person who summons up the energy and courage to ask, "Why do I get up on Monday morning?", there are many who hope that more busyness will feed their hunger, who plod on—waiting. Waiting for some special person or event to point the way. Waiting, perhaps, to be called.

A good place to start with our purpose exploration is at the core with the courageous question, "Why *do* I get up on Monday morning?" For many of us, reflection on this question is as tough as it is inevitable. Ideally, we should not let a day pass without spending some time revitalizing the spiritual in us. Eventually, we really listen to our deepest calling, and there is an enormous hunger for that.

We need to ask ourselves what we really need in our lives. A real need is something we must have to survive. After our basic needs are clear, we begin to look at our wants. Wants enrich the quality of our lives. What we truly want often reflects our purpose.

Psychologist Abraham Maslow arranged human needs into a hierarchy. He claimed that our basic needs must be at least minimally fulfilled before we can move toward our wants. Our physical needs (e.g. air, food, shelter) are the most basic. These needs must be satisfied before we can free our energies to pursue needs at the next level, and so on. As Gandhi said, "Even God cannot talk to a hungry man except in terms of bread."

At the next level, according to Maslow, we must feel minimally safe and secure in our day-to-day activities. We all define safety and security in different ways. Our fundamental need to feel that our life and our work are rooted in solid ground is essential.

At the next level, we must feel a sense of companionship and affection. We need love—some kind of recognition that we have worth, that someone cares. Our self-worth can be badly damaged by lack of real love. Self-worth will rise if we engage in life and work activities that we believe are worthwhile, in which we can be contributing members of society. To the extent that we spend our precious time currency on activities that we don't value, that we consider "worthless," our self-worth will diminish.

As Maslow stated, "Even if all these needs are satisfied, we may still often (if not always) expect that a new discontent and restlessness will soon develop unless the individual is doing what he is fitted for. A musician must make music, an artist must paint, a writer must write if he is to be ultimately at peace with himself. What a man can be, he must be. This need we call self-actualization."

At the highest level, we operate with purpose. At this level we are growing, stretching, and utilizing our highest gifts and talents. We have a clear answer for the question, "Why do I get up on Monday morning?"

Stop for a moment and ask yourself: "Why *do* I get up on Monday morning?" Repeat the question several times out loud.

CHAPTER 6

THE PURPOSE SPIRAL

We are all on a spiral path. No growth takes place in a straight line.
There will be setbacks along the way. . . . There will be shadows,
but they will be balanced by patches of light. . . .
Awareness of the pattern is all you need to sustain you along the way.

—KRISTIN ZAMBUCKA

All life is a spiral of change, a constant graceful curve toward purpose. There is a definite pattern to it all. And we spend our whole lives seeking that pattern by discovering different questions at different ages and stages. Searching for the pattern is the heart of our human quest. If we're aware of that pattern, and where we are in it, we can identify the best choices to sustain us along the way.

Most of us find that our purpose evolves as experiences evolve over our lifetimes. A new sense of purpose is triggered by age, by crisis, and by a natural, ongoing discovery of who we are. It is part of the quest for purpose to ask new questions as we age.

If living on purpose sounds like an impractical order, think about a spiral. The Random House unabridged *Dictionary of the*

English Language defines a spiral as "running continually around a fixed point or center while
constantly receding from or approaching it."
The spiral projects the image of a continuity
that coils in one plane—like a chambered nautilus—around one particular center.

There is a clear analogy between the evolu-
tion of purpose and the natural evolution of a chambered nautilus
shell. Each has a basic center of orientation that provides a coherent
pattern of growth. Initially, the nautilus occupies only the smallest
chamber at the center of the spiral. That is the whole shell. From its
core, the nautilus keeps adding new chambers throughout its life as
it needs more space to grow.

The nautilus is in the natural shape of a spiral. Think of your
life as a nautilus with many chambers behind you and many ahead,
yet to be added. Each chamber has an opening and an emerging chan-
nel to the chamber next to it.

The nautilus is a natural pattern for discovering our purpose
in today's world. As we, too, move through different phases, or chambers, our purpose evolves. The old chambers feel cramped and lack
room to stretch and breathe. We outgrow people, places, and purposes. We move into new chambers to make way for the new to
emerge.

As Pat Murphy and William Neill see it in their book *By
Nature's Design*: "Life more often than not does not draw straight
lines. The world is filled with graceful curves—from the elegant spiral in the heart of the nautilus shell to the twisting double helix of
DNA that codes for the nautilus' growth."

Each life has its own special design. There is a pattern of growth
in which we all are involved. We naturally find ourselves at different
ages looking in different directions and asking different questions.

We do not remain children forever but rather move through various cycles toward wisdom and maturity.

Discovering the pattern is what it means to be human. Life is a continuous spiral of lessons to be learned as we grow back toward our birth source. We grow through chambers of progressive awakenings that involve physical, mental, emotional, and spiritual transitions.

Life is a quest—a series of questions to be answered. If you look back and examine the past chambers of your life, each contained a natural yet tough question. And as you lived in the tough questions, they taught you the essential truths of life and showed you new questions.

Each transition to a new chamber of purpose is accompanied by a crisis of uncertainty, a chaotic period of time in which we are organizing ourselves around a new core question.

The secret to a fully alive life is learning how to reframe our life questions over and over, letting go of what is no longer relevant, and taking on new questions guided by our evolving purpose. Each chamber is naturally important as a basis for further growth.

Core Questions

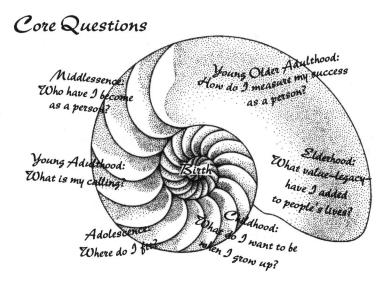

Middlessence:
Who have I become
as a person?

Young Older Adulthood:
How do I measure my success
as a person?

Young Adulthood:
What is my calling?

Birth

Elderhood:
What value-legacy
have I added
to people's lives?

Childhood:
What do I want to be
when I grow up?

Adolescence:
Where do I fit?

A growing number of people are expecting their work to provide daily meaning and daily bread. They want work that integrates their unique gifts and talents with the practical realities of surviving and making a living.

At age 26, Andrew Leider, like many his age, wants both meaning and bread. "What's your purpose?" I asked Andrew over coffee one morning. He quickly responded, "To make my way in the world without losing myself!"

After college, Andrew never intended to live what he calls "a tract life." He was not looking for what he'd do for the next 40 years. While many of his friends were purposefully becoming lawyers, doctors, ministers, and businesspeople, he was enjoying a different quest and different questions. His core question was, "What am I willing to trade my time for without compromising my values?"

Based on his passions and values, he gravitated to the wilderness adventure-learning-based Outward Bound schools. The purpose of Outward Bound is to conduct safe, adventure-based programs structured to inspire self-esteem, self-reliance, concern for others, and care for the environment. As an Outward Bound instructor, Andrew studies it intensely and has discovered a natural gift for leading wilderness courses. He says, "Outward Bound fulfills my personality for the predictable future. Although I'm not making much money, I am able to survive nicely and integrate who I am with what I do."

The magic of Outward Bound for Andrew is that it is a place that consciously supports the integration of his work and his life. It is a blessing for him, because it gives him the opportunity early in life to experience the integrity of surviving without compromising his values.

Management consultant Peter Drucker described our career choices as "The probability that the first choice you make is right for you is roughly one in a million. If you decide that your first choice was the right one, chances are you are just plain lazy." Everything we do builds toward our next life chamber and the evolution of our purpose. Rarely do we have wasted work, though at the time it might seem that way. We're always growing and mastering life's lessons, even hard to recognize ones, that move us forward on purpose.

The integration of who we are with what we do is one of the true joys in life. We're all challenged to shape and create the specific and unique way we are going to do the work we are called to do. Discovering our calling means living our values. It means putting our values to work by resolving to make what we do reflect who we really are.

From early childhood, we are taught to behave in ways that fit the purposes of others. As children, we are naturally open, yet dependent on the lead set by others. To follow the lead of our parents, peers, teachers, etc., provides us with approval. Sooner or later we realize it is easier to base our choices on "what is expected of us" rather than on "what is meaningful to us." Sometimes we become so dependent on these external standards that we no longer know what we truly need or want.

Many of us wait for something to happen. We spend much of our life waiting. What a strange hold this waiting has on us. Waiting for a sign. Waiting to be called. Not committing ourselves to anything until everything is right. Waiting for the grand opportunity, when our full gifts and talents will be unleashed and used.

Waiting by its very nature traps us in a way of living that makes our life superficial and disappointing. We do not know where to turn to find fulfillment in life. Because we find so little fulfillment within ourselves, we may look for happiness and self-worth in material possessions and social success.

In *The Overworked American,* economist Juliet Schor describes "the squirrel cage of work and spend" that traps so many people. "Happiness," she claims, "has failed to keep pace with economic growth." No matter how much we make, it is never enough. There is a false belief that "the next purchase will yield happiness, and then the next."

If we find no joy in the work we do, then we are set up for the "squirrel cage" mentality of "work, and spend, and work and spend some more."

All of us want the best out of life. We want to be happy and to have things that can enrich our experience. Yet, though we strive for these things, we end up unfulfilled. We may have a good life. But if we do not discover our purpose, then a large portion of each day is spent doing something we do not truly care about and would rather not be doing. We may spend so much of our lives waiting that we never awaken to the true joy of purposeful living. The spiral will end. Death will claim us, and we will not have had more than a moment of contentment.

One of the requirements of discovering our calling is to come face to face with the sacred, mysterious part of ourselves. And to do that we must make friends with death. Living and working on purpose means facing squarely the questions of mortality: "Where did I come from?" "Where am I going to?" "What's my reason for being here, now?" "What is my calling?" "Who is doing the calling?"

Bailey Allard is an executive development consultant and professional speaker who often tells stories of her grandmother, Berteen Bailey. Her grandmother taught her that "as long as we can laugh and joke, life is worth living." Bailey says, "I believe the glass is totally full! I'm born. I breathe. I walk. I have my whiny days, but I have the skills of how to make it funny; to see the positive in things. I learned from my grandmother how to make every day fun!"

Bailey's eyes burn with intensity and fire as she recalls this story about her grandmother's influence on her: "It was a 'mother's ring.' You know, the kind set with the birthstone of every child born to the mother. This mother's ring belonged to my grandmother. Four stones. Three children still living. She had worn the ring for years. Then, one day, without warning, it was gone. Inadvertently the small gold band had slipped off her gnarled, arthritic fingers. She looked everywhere and instantly knew she had lost it in the yard somewhere. That was two years ago. Two years, searching, still no ring. She died last week. On the morning of her funeral, one of her grandsons found the ring in the driveway, as if it magically appeared at his feet. Unfinished business? 'Just one more thing to do before I go,' I can almost hear her laugh."

Bailey's life combines her grandmother's philosophy: "As long as we can laugh and joke, life is worth living" with her own purpose of "helping people learn and leverage their unique gifts." She believes we're all spiritually guided and that part of true enlightenment is to "lighten up" and find something funny in every single day. Like her grandmother, she believes that laughter keeps us going and that laughter is part of her own legacy as well. Bailey relates, "I can't, at age 48, afford to hold back any longer. I have no patience for work that I can't bring life to or that is not fun!"

Death can be a purposeful force. The highest values of life can originate from brushing up against it. Squarely facing our own mortality lets us take a fresh approach, and ask the big questions. It can shatter old assumptions and generate new questions.

Ernest Becker, in *The Denial of Death*, claims, "The fear of death is the basic fear that influences all others; a fear from which no one is immune no matter how disguised it may be." Rollo May adds, "The confronting of death gives the most positive reality to life itself. It makes the individual existence real, absolute, and concrete. Death is the one fact of my life which is not relative but absolute and my awareness of this gives my existence and what I do each hour an absolute quality."

Few express no anxiety about death. In *The Art of Dying*, Robert F. Neale considers our fears of death:

Fear of what happens after death

- Fate of my body—idea that my physical body will decay
- The unknown that follows—the unendingness of eternity

Fear of the process of dying

- The pain—the final struggle
- Indignity—the humiliation of giving up control of bodily functions
- Being a burden—few of us will die by accident; becoming a physical, emotional, or financial burden

Fear of the loss of life

- Loss of mastery—end of our control over life
- Incompleteness and failure—not tasting, experiencing, learning, achieving all we intended to
- Separation—being taken from those we love; sorrow and hardship to family and friends

Purpose is immortal. To face death squarely is to face purpose squarely. Mysteriously, the creative spirit of the universe calls us at various times and in various ways to make our own difference in the work of the universe—to fulfill our own special design.

Look back over the chambers of your own life spiral. What were your core questions during each phase of your life? What is your core question today?

CHAPTER 7

AN ALIVENESS QUESTIONNAIRE

What we are seeking is an experience of being alive,
so that we actually feel the rapture of being alive.

—JOSEPH CAMPBELL

Each life is an experiment of one. There is no other human being on earth with your unique purpose. Each of us must shape our own quest to discover our purpose. Exploring our quality of life, our "experience of being alive," will help us become more conscious of our quest.

Jim Channon embodies aliveness. He lives a radically different timeprint and integrates an amazing variety of things into his life. In his purpose quest, he follows a "be all you can be" philosophy, harkening back to his military career. In exploring the work arenas of visual language, strategic design, military tactics, corporate strategy, tribal cultures, geomythology, and the human spirit, he follows the path of an adventure shaman.

Jim asks, "When in our lifetime do we ever really have a chance to know ourselves?" To help answer that question for himself and others, Jim's purpose is "to help people know themselves as they are gifted by life with a deep calling . . . to be played out to its fullest in the moment that counts."

Jim's calling has led him to become a social architect, corporate visioning and learning guide. He has advised ten of the world's largest corporations on their strategic direction and corporate cultures. In the army, the first of four careers to date, he led paratroopers in combat and commanded the First Earth Battalion, a 21st-century prototype of the soldier of the future.

He has mastered a unique process for coaching out the very deepest potential in a person or a corporation and then parading that essence forward in drawings and dramatic stories. In his Passage to Destiny retreats, people are encouraged to bring forth the many sources of their natural talents. Jim says, "In life, we are first fragments of our parents, then models of the prevailing social system, and maybe if we're lucky working in a profession that draws somewhat upon that inner wealth we have at our core. In only the rarest of moments is our natural genius surfaced and expressed."

What are the signs that indicate that you "actually feel the rapture of being alive"? What are the signs that indicate that, no, your life isn't as full and vital as you might wish? Think of answering the following Aliveness Questionnaire as you would a periodic physical examination. Check either Yes or No according to how you feel about each question today.

The total number of "Yes" responses on the Aliveness Questionnaire provides a general sense of your aliveness. A high number indicates that you have deep life energy. You might actually feel "the rapture of being alive."

As you reflect on your "aliveness," focus on the questions you need to pay more attention to. In the following discussion, decide

An Aliveness Questionnaire	Yes	No
1. Do I feel a sense of balance in my life?	_____	_____
2. Do I regularly enjoy hearty belly laughs?	_____	_____
3. Do I live my dreams?	_____	_____
4. Do I take time for solitude?	_____	_____
5. Do I have at least two nutritious people in my life?	_____	_____
6. Do I feel the energy of optimum health?	_____	_____
7. Do I have a spiritual practice in my life?	_____	_____
8. Do I feel that my life matters?	_____	_____
9. Does my recreation time re-create me?	_____	_____
10. Do I have the courage to say "No"?	_____	_____

Total "Yes" Responses = _____

whether you want to take action to modify your habits. No one has mastered all these factors. Everyone experiences self-doubts and ups and downs. Aliveness does not mean perfection! It does mean a willingness to live life openly and fully, acknowledging your humanness. Remember to give yourself credit where you've done well.

The Aliveness Questionnaire is an opportunity to reflect. Take some solitude time, after your initial scoring, to contemplate further about each of the questions.

QUESTION 1:
DO I FEEL A SENSE OF BALANCE IN MY LIFE?

In my work as a career coach, I often must deal with the fallout from imbalanced lives; problems with children, marital strains, and stress illnesses. The imbalance between home and work time is often the most common subject of off-line work conversations. There is a deep hunger for balance in the work world.

Each of us must decide what the proper balance formula is for our own lives. In doing so, it is important to understand that we tend to define our lives by what we do. For example, the first question people often ask is, "What do you do?" and through our answer they compare themselves with us. This gives them a frame of reference to continue (or discontinue) the discussion. Work is important to our identity. It is dangerous, however, to claim all of our self-worth through our vocation, title, or business card.

Three of the currencies we have to spend in life are time, talents, and money.

Money can be spent and re-earned; we can lose all of our savings or our job and then come back again and take another shot at it. Time, however, is the most precious currency of life, and how we spend it reflects what we truly value. Once we have spent it, it is gone forever! It cannot be re-earned. Are you feeling in charge of the time in your life?

QUESTION 2:
DO I REGULARLY ENJOY HEARTY BELLY LAUGHS?

We have gotten so serious in our culture! We have forgotten how to laugh and be joyous. In fact, it is estimated that one out of three people will probably need assistance to work their way out of some kind of depression within their lifetime.

While this question uses the term *belly laughs*, it really refers to playfulness. Playfulness is a frame of mind.

There is a direct connection between playfulness and health. If a negative mind can make the body sick, then what can make it well?

Obviously, positive thoughts, such as playfulness and humor. Play is a primary need in life. Set yourself a goal to have one good belly laugh per day. When you start looking for humor in your life, you will often find it. A perspective of playfulness is increasingly important as we move through stressful events. Think of hearty belly laughs as internal jogging and ponder this: "He or she who laughs . . . lasts!" Are you having much fun these days?

QUESTION 3:
DO I LIVE MY DREAMS?

How many people do you know can truthfully say they live, for the most part, the way they truly want to live? Can you say that you do?

It has become popular for people to talk about the future—the 21st century, the next millennium. Probably fewer than 10 people out of 100 have written down any plans for their future.

If you had 200 years to live, you might not have to do much planning. However, we must look at the fact that we have only so many years to live. Thus, we must order our priorities accordingly. Often the trickiest part of getting what we want out of life is "figuring out what it is we want." When you ask people, "What do you want out of life?" it often boils down to two things: work and love.

As Henry David Thoreau said, "If a man advances confidently in the direction of his dreams to live the life he has imagined, he will meet with a success unexpected in common hours." Are you living your dreams?

QUESTION 4:
DO I TAKE TIME FOR SOLITUDE?

This question came from a variety of sources, one of which is the Outward Bound Wilderness Schools where the "solo"—a 24-hour or more time of solitude—is a part of the program. Many people are frightened by the solo before they begin it. After they return, however, many think that the solo was the highlight of their entire adventure. You don't have to go to the wilderness to take a solo; you can take a mini-solo of 10 to 15 minutes each day.

Since busyness is a status symbol in our society, even our leisure time is heavily scheduled. All of this busyness leads to noisy minds and keeps us from knowing our feelings and inner self. We need to make regular appointments with ourselves—solos—to make sure that we are paying attention to what's important in our lives. When is the last time you stopped long enough to step back and look at the big picture of your life?

QUESTION 5:
DO I HAVE AT LEAST TWO
NUTRITIOUS PEOPLE IN MY LIFE?

We all are forced to deal with toxic people in our lives—people who make us feel worse after we are with them than if we had not been with them at all. To offset this, we need "nutritious" people in our lives. Nutritious people have three primary characteristics: their face lights up when you come in the room, they listen to you, and they have few (i.e., no) plans for your improvement!

We all need a good support network in the world we are living in today, and nutritious people need to be part of our networks. Who are the two most nutritious people in your life?

QUESTION 6:
DO I FEEL THE ENERGY OF OPTIMUM HEALTH?

The idea behind the Aliveness Questionnaire is that "you don't have to be sick to get better." This certainly holds true for our health. We need to learn to pay attention to our bodily signals, which tell us how we are doing and how we are feeling. We pay the price either now or later, as far as our health goes.

Aristotle's advice was sound when he said, "Be a good animal first." We need to pay attention to our aerobic capacity, flexibility, strength, relaxation, nutrition, and sleep patterns, as well as to our life philosophies and purposes. Do you have the energy to do the things you love to do?

QUESTION 7:
DO I HAVE A SPIRITUAL PRACTICE IN MY LIFE?

We need to pay attention in our lives to the "imponderables"—our spiritual core. Even Einstein, for all of his scientific wisdom, came to the conclusion "I cannot believe that God plays dice with the cosmos."

Throughout our lives, we regularly feel three "hungers": (1) the hunger for meaning, for leaving footprints, and for having our lives recognized as worthwhile; (2) the hunger for intimacy and community, to be cared about, and to give and receive love; and (3) the hunger for self—to grow, to understand our uniqueness, and to figure out how to most effectively use our gifts during our short lifetime. We need a regular practice to help feed our spiritual hunger. Do you have a spiritual practice—meditation, prayer, contemplation—that feeds your hunger?

QUESTION 8:
DO I FEEL THAT MY LIFE MATTERS?

Purpose does not mean winning the Nobel Prize or creating world-shaking inventions, life-saving exploits, artistic triumphs, or even raising millions for cancer, as Terry Fox did. The simple truth is that we all just need to feel we matter.

Gandhi's life is an obvious example of a life that mattered. This remarkable man changed the world. The world laughed at him when he set out to free India and her millions from the yoke of British colonialism; but that's precisely what he did. And isn't it interesting that the people who truly change the world often have no armies to help them!

Are you feeling that you're making a creative contribution to life—that, should you die prematurely, you're leaving a legacy?

QUESTION 9:
DOES MY RECREATION TIME RE-CREATE ME?

Often we treat ourselves as machines that need refueling rather than as living beings who have natural rhythms of our own. The notion here of recreation indicates a frame of mind for doing something "just for the sake of doing it" (not to achieve anything)! Children know how to play, to do something naturally essential to good mental health. Many of us need to relearn how to re-create. What are the ways you really have "fun"?

When was the last time you engaged in these fun things?

QUESTION 10:
DO I HAVE THE COURAGE TO SAY "NO"?

Many of us have systems that we use at work for managing our responsibilities and priorities. How well do you manage your personal time priorities on a day-to-day basis?

Managing one's time currency with clear boundaries is essential in today's busy environment. Balancing work and home demands is one of the major stressors today. The balance between work and home is often where problems occur. Contrary to many people's thinking, to be organized often means the liberation of time and energy, not the cramping of our style.

An airline pilot usually goes through a checklist just before takeoff and just before landing. We need the same sort of process—a checklist of sorts to keep ourselves in touch with our life priorities. What process do you use to decide what to say "yes" and what to say "no" to in your daily life?

People who answered yes to most of the questions on the Aliveness Questionnaire are not paragons of virtue. The fact is that they are just as concerned with inner life as with outer life. They are people who have made tough choices about their balance, their dreams, their health, their relationships, and their time. They come from a place inside themselves to define what their boundaries are. Aliveness can only be self-measured. In fact, others may not even notice, because aliveness is not a superior state of being—it's a feeling.

CHAPTER 8

THE RUSTOUT SYNDROME

Compared with what we ought to be, we are only half awake.

—WILLIAM JAMESL

We need stress. However, it goes without saying that we should not be subjected to too much stress. In the United States, stress-related diseases cost the U.S. economy $200 billion per year in absenteeism and medical expenses. The United Nations International Labor Organization labels job stress "a global phenomenon—one of the most serious health issues of the twentieth century." Too much stress is deadly.

What we need is the right amount of the right kind of stress. Not only too-great demands, but also the opposite—the lack of challenges—may cause disease.

What we need is a creative tension, or tension between a person and a purpose he or she wants to fulfill. We are not just in search of stress per se, but, in particular, in search of tasks whose completion will add meaning to our lives. Today, however, many of us are not finding much meaning. Psychotherapists and counselors report that a major complaint they hear day in and day out is a feeling of futility and emptiness. Its main symptom is purposelessness, which often comes from the lack of a spiritual sense of work.

Pervasive cynicism and boredom are attitudes toward life held by many people today. Take for example the vice president of a high-technology company whom I coach. "I just can't seem to get going," the vice president said. "I used to be an up-and-coming salesman with this company. Now I can't get interested in what I'm supposed to do. I know I should get rolling. I'm sleepwalking through the day. And I'm awake at night. I'm going to the liquor store twice a week. Once used to be enough. I feel trapped!"

In short, he was rusting out. He felt trapped in a kind of vocational quicksand. He was not challenged. He felt he could not leave, nor could he succeed.

He went on to say, "I don't know how much longer I can last in this job. I've been with the company for fifteen years and have changed jobs every two to three years. The organization charts keep changing, but the politics don't. We're still being told what we must do and when. The old virtues of initiative and taking risks are not being rewarded. The process of getting rewards is more political now. I'm demoralized."

What was happening to this executive? He felt that no one cared about the contribution he was making. That caused him to raise the question "What for?"—as if he'd lost sight of his purpose for getting up in the morning.

Most people probably experience rustout at some point in their lives. If a person is not challenged by meaningful tasks and is spared the positive stress surrounding such tasks, rustout occurs. It is the condition of not using our gifts toward some end that moves us. The key is to find a need in our world that needs doing and decide to fill it. In so doing, we discover our own calling, our unique way of adding value to the planet.

Doug Donovan felt he was rusting out. He needed a change. When he left his corporate job, he was given a beautiful sculpture of a soaring eagle. One year later at a safari camp near the Serengeti Plains of Tanzania, he was asked to figure out a metaphor for his life. Into his consciousness came the metaphor of a soaring eagle. He wrote in his journal: "I need a higher, broader perspective. I believe I'm good at visioning the possibilities. I am private, a little remote, one with the circling wind. When I spot an opportunity, I dive from the skies for it."

When he returned home, he looked up the eagle symbol in a book of Native American symbols called *Medicine Cards*. He learned that "when you call upon the power of an animal, you are asking to be drawn into complete harmony with the strength of the creature's essence. Eagle Medicine is the power of the Great Spirit. It's the ability to live in the realm of Spirit, and yet remain connected and balanced within the realm of Earth. . . . A soaring eagle means you are being put on notice of a need to reconnect with the higher mind."

After becoming ever more aware of his metaphor, Doug became very conscious of a song in his church service entitled "On Eagles' Wings." The refrain in the song was "And He will raise you up on eagles' wings . . .".

At a personal-growth seminar, Doug wrote, "My purpose is to become as much as I can be and to help others become as much as they can be . . . to reach out and touch the minds and hearts and spirits of others . . . to soar like an eagle, seek a higher vision and to help the human spirit to soar to its potential . . . to its purpose . . . to its Maker."

The power of picking a metaphor can be an effective technique for renewing our sense of aliveness. It can provide a tangible day-to-day reminder of our purpose. Can you think of a symbol or metaphor for your life?

Rustout is similar to a garden in which nothing grows—it's empty. Life lacks purpose; nothing moves us. There is nothing to explore that might open us to our own aliveness. Our work lacks promise; life continues day by day at the same petty pace. Helen Keller said, "Life is either a daring adventure or nothing." Rustout is when life has become the latter.

Like generalized stress, rustout cuts across all ages and levels. People in these situations feel chronic fatigue, anger, self-criticism, and indifference. They can no longer invest themselves in others or in their work. Everyone knows the phenomenon of being more or less awake on different days. With rustout, our talents are slumbering.

We need to wake up to our potential for higher forms of purpose. But how can we awaken? How can we escape this sleep? Do we need a periodic wake-up call? We usually do not wake up by ourselves. It often takes another person, more awake than ourselves, to give us a periodic wake-up call. Without a person like this, we often need a major crisis to get our attention.

Who awakens you? Who gives you that periodic wake-up call to the possibilities your life holds?

Despite an almost universal belief to the contrary, the pursuit of happiness as it is interpreted today is a myth. Ease, comfort, and a state of having arrived do not constitute happiness for most human beings.

The fact is that satisfaction always leads to dissatisfaction! A life without challenge and difficulty leads to a sparse and shallow existence. Comfort and leisure are great, but they're just not enough. If this were the case, the large number of us who enjoy relative affluence would be ecstatically happy!

The true story of happiness involves living and working on purpose. Purpose helps us focus on the deepest, widest questions of our being.

So, if society offers us too little of the right kind of stress, we start creating it—the very stress we have been spared. We deliberately place demands on ourselves by voluntarily exposing ourselves to stress situations, if only temporarily. Some people choose extreme sports like rock climbing, race car driving, helicopter skiing, and the like to bring them the aliveness that is often missing in their life and work.

Many would argue that helping or expressing goodwill toward others provides a greater sense of positive stress. Hans Selye has suggested that the way to enjoy a rewarding lifestyle, free of disabling stress, is to practice "altruistic egoism." In essence, this involves helping others by working on purpose.

Selye points out that our biological nature drives us toward self-preservation, or what might commonly be called selfishness. Selye's line of thought suggests that only by linking this self-centered innate nature with an attitude of earning the goodwill and respect of others through altruistic efforts will a happy, meaningful life result.

We may never fully understand our altruistic urge, let alone human nature, but the heart of purpose is centered in the simple idea of caring for our fellow human beings (and ourselves, in the process).

We can choose to make our caring for each other what our lives are all about. The challenge is for us to find what kind of caring provides that feeling of aliveness we seek. Purpose is at the heart of our search.

PART III

WORKING ON PURPOSE

CHAPTER 9

ARE YOU HEARING YOUR CALLING?

Our deepest fear is not that we are inadequate,
Our deepest fear is that we are powerful beyond measure

—MARIANNE WILLIAMSON

What are your expectations of your work? Is work something to be suffered through and endured? Or is work synonymous with a calling?

A calling is about working with meaning, joy, and a sense of contributing to the greater community. A calling means bringing spirit and livelihood back together again. A calling calls forth the deeper questions of work, such as how, why, and for whom we do our work.

Earlier in our history, people offered their daily activities as a "thank you" to God, because all enterprise was ultimately intended for God. This was the basis for the infamous work ethic. The concept of stewardship, by which one made an offering to God of one's best efforts, elevated a person's work to the status of a calling.

The most obvious thing about purpose from the point of view of calling is that it is connected to the concept of stewardship. Every individual is by creation essentially a steward. And this is possible because each of us has been born with certain unique gifts. We are accountable to God for how they are used, misused, or not used at all.

Nelson Mandela's inaugural speech upon assuming the presidency of South Africa had a profound effect on Phil Styrlund's concept of stewardship. The part that stuck with him was a quote from Marianne Williamson's book, *A Return to Love:*

> Our deepest fear is not that we are inadequate. Our deepest fear is that we are powerful beyond measure. It is our light, not our darkness, that most frightens us. We ask ourselves, Who am I to be brilliant, gorgeous, talented, fabulous? Actually, who are you not to be? You are a child of God. Your playing small doesn't serve the world. There's nothing enlightened about shrinking so that other people won't feel insecure around you. We are all meant to shine, as children do. We were born to make manifest the glory of God that is within us. It's not just in some of us; it's in everyone. And as we let our own light shine, we unconsciously give other people permission to do the same. As we're liberated from our own fear, our presence automatically liberates others.

Phil had long believed that there is something grand going on in the world—that we're living in a mystery grander than we as humans are able to comprehend. And he had a hunger, a calling, to play larger in that world.

Phil has a stream-of-consciousness work style. He says, "I'm never sure if I'm working or not. I don't view my work as work; it's just me in other settings. As a result, I have trouble with weekends. I get anxious on Sunday night to get on to the next phase of my work."

As a senior vice president of a large telecommunications company, Phil has the privilege of being paid to do something that he likes to do for free. He claims, "It's only through relationships that anything significant and sustainable can be achieved. As a leader, I find pleasure, beyond comprehension, being a small part of making other people's lives big. My purpose is to enlarge and dignify the lives of others." Phil has a personal calling to create an environment of psychological safety where people can speak their truth and express their gifts. He says, "Productivity is a natural outcome of using your gifts in a healthy environment."

Phil believes that the power of leadership is the power of asking and living in questions. "As a leader," he says, "I collect questions!" The two most powerful questions that inform his leadership are "Why are we here?" and "Where are we going?" Through these and other questions, Phil has shaped a distinct and successful leadership philosophy he calls "purposeful selfishness." To clarify this, he returns to Mandela's speech: "As we are liberated from our fear, our presence automatically liberates others." As a leader, he believes, he must work on liberating himself in order to hear his calling.

After many years as a career coach, I have come to the conclusion that many people perceive their work in one of two ways: they are devoted to work for strictly financial ends, or they have a sense of purpose that is not consistent with the purpose of the organization for whom they work. In short, many people do not connect deeply with their work. And judging by the dramatic rise in the number of stress-related problems among workers at all levels, many feel alienated from any meaning in their work.

Toward what end do so many strive? The work ethic is obviously not dead or even dying. For some, it is the advancement of our own careers. We will make tremendous sacrifices for it, will bend over backward to avoid *making waves* to advance it, and will treat ourselves as resumés to be *packaged* and *marketed* to further it. The consequence of such an orientation to work is that we begin to view work as a consumer; to become motivated primarily by personal gain—what it will get us. The result is a workforce with highly refined skills of the head, but not of the heart.

James Autry got it right when he wrote, "Work can provide the opportunity for spiritual and personal as well as financial growth. If it doesn't, we're wasting far too much of our lives on it." We are tired of working for organizations that consume us and offer money in return for stressful and unfulfilling work.

In a global, high-tech, reengineered work world, many people today are forced to reconsider the merits of conventional success—such as security, advancement, and retirement—and are beginning to place higher value on stewardship criteria, such as closeness to God, family, community, and nature.

My career coaching work involves helping people become clearer about the presence or absence of meaning in their work. Since becoming passionate about the importance and benefits of purpose in work, I have made a practice of interviewing people I meet who seem "called to" their work. This helps to test my hypothesis that true joy is associated with a connection to some higher purpose or calling.

Of course, I have observed many people reporting to work every day who are cynical and rusted-out, who have given up and who seem content to make it to quitting time. Many people genuinely feel overworked. They are, in the words of German mystic Meister Eckhart, "worked" instead of working. Many feel that although they still believe it to be ethically important for them to work hard, they don't see any social or personal benefit deriving from their work.

People who perform most energetically, creatively, and enthusiastically are those who believe they are contributing to a purpose outside of and larger than themselves. They have a calling. The failure of many organizations to enlist people in some kind of unselfish, nonquantitative purpose is at the root of many productivity problems today. When we ignore purpose at work, we inhibit the highest motivator.

Hearing a calling—a work mission that goes beyond oneself—has many productive consequences. It provides us with a source of deep energy. We are clear as to how others may benefit from our efforts. It provides principles for our conduct. It provides a focus for spending our precious time meaningfully.

A missing piece in much work training is a process for helping people hear their calling, a process that helps people:

- identify their most enjoyed gifts and talents.

- give their gifts in service of some issue, product, or service they care about.

- identify work environments that fit "who they are"—their values.

The notion of hearing our calling may take a while to digest. It requires an openness of the heart and—above all—patience. The discovery of our calling often requires an incubation period. The architect LeCorbusier said that the birth of a project was just like the birth of a child: "There's a long period of gestation . . . a lot of work in the subconscious before I make the first sketch. That lasts for months. One fine morning the project has taken form without my knowing it."

Most of us want to feel that we are significant and that our work calls us to something enduring and worthwhile. More than anything else, good work enables us to spend our precious time in ways consistent with our calling in life.

CHAPTER 10

DAILY MEANING AND DAILY BREAD

This book is about a search, too, for daily meaning as well as daily bread,
for recognition as well as cash, for astonishment rather than torpor;
in short, for a sort of life rather than a Monday through Friday sort of dying.

—STUDS TERKEL

One of the first experiences of my professional career was a conference I attended shortly after I began my first full-time position. I was excited to meet new colleagues and have an opportunity to hear some esteemed thinkers in my field, people whom I had only read of previously. Many of us new to the field listened attentively to one of the foremost authorities deliver a rather dismal keynote address. We were told that we could look forward to increasing workloads, red tape, and a race against obsolescence. His comments were underscored by other speakers—that we must be prepared for the worst. Suddenly I had a sinking feeling about my chosen path.

I have remembered that experience on more than one occasion. Because these were extremely competent people, I was quite disturbed by the message conveyed. My problem with what was presented was that it strongly suggested that the path to work success involved a joyless struggle.

We have a need to find joy in our work. To the extent that we use our most enjoyed gifts on the situations that hold special interest for us, we build joy into our work. To the extent that we pursue worthwhile challenges that we feel natural passion for, an inner purpose is activated. The way to be effective and find joy and meaning through our work is to discover what is needed and wanted, and then produce it—right where we are! Discovering that principle, we also discover that who we are matters. We do count. The work we do does make a difference. We can plan our work so that we enjoyably progress toward our desired success. In fact, it's legitimate to enjoy what we're doing!

The Heartland Institute has as its mission "the integration of personal growth and social transformation to cultivate healthier individuals, families, workplaces and communities." Heartland's co-founder, Craig Neal, helps achieve this through the development of local and national learning events and related consulting and publishing ventures.

Craig recalls, "I've always been fascinated by the big questions of purpose, values, and consciousness. In fact, I remember the day I first thought about my purpose, during the 1963 March on Washington. There I was, standing right in front of the Lincoln Memorial during Martin Luther King's 'I Have a Dream' speech. That speech shifted my life, forever. I went from an oblivious 16-year-old suburban New Jersey high school kid to a spiritual seeker."

During Craig's ensuing 20-year career, he sought to work only for organizations and people who had strong values. He eventually joined Garden Way, an organization dedicated to saving the world through gardening, and he also worked on founding the Harrowsmith and Organic Gardening publications.

He came to an awakening during his 5-year stint as publisher of the *Utne Reader* that business is the most powerful force for change on the planet. "What hit me," Craig recalled, "is that everyone works and that the purpose of work was to provide a service. I was happiest when I was serving others or working in companies whose service aided the natural evolution of the planet."

Craig's natural inclination was to start organizing around "the big questions." So he got involved with emerging organizations like Business for Social Responsibility and Social Venture Network. He began to see more clearly how many people didn't know how to "serve and make a living." He saw how they compromised for so much less than they knew they could give to their work.

Craig's missionary zeal caused him to become increasingly impatient—wanting it all to work in this world, now. He recalled a friend from his earlier years asking him, "Why are you always so earnest?" His reply was, "I'm a cross between Sol Alinsky (an organizer with feet on the ground) and Meher Baba (a mystic pondering the imponderables)."

Today, Craig Neal is a "mystic organizer." His purpose is to be of service, to be useful while he's here. "My purpose," Craig states emphatically, "is to develop ways so people can share their personal gifts with their organizations, and organizations can nurture and give back to their workers." Craig reflects on his journey, "What it all boils down to is courage. It's not mystical; it's practical. If the human spirit already, as I believe, embodies everything, the question is one of courage. What am I willing to do, at this moment?"

The Heartland Institute supports courage in the workplace. Through learning events like The Inner Life of Business and associates like the Conscious Business Alliance, Craig and his wife Patricia are steering the Heartland Institute toward an important role in the 21st century. Part mystics and part organizers, they are driving themselves and others to seek and to follow their calling.

Andrew Stirrat wanted, more than anything else, to travel and explore new lands. So, recalling the advice his father gave him—"If you're not doing what you love to do, now, you may never experience what you really want to do"—he hit the road.

He hiked the Pacific Crest Trail, drove the length of Africa, lived on a Kibbutz in Israel, trekked through Asia, kayaked in the Arctic, and biked and backpacked throughout the United States. In between adventures, he worked as a contractor/laborer to build his bank account for the next escape.

After following his bliss for 15 years, he decided it was time to settle into an appropriate career using the learnings from his travels. He became an instructor for Outward Bound and found that many adults were coming to programs seeking the same sense of adventure that he had been pursuing much of his life.

Andrew began using the outdoors as a metaphor for life's learning experiences, to help people rediscover themselves. Today, he creates environments where people can take risks. As a founding partner of Headwaters Leadership Group, he inspires and helps people find new ways to lead themselves and their organizations into the 21st century. Andrew's purpose today is: "To help people grow and rediscover their essence."

Through his own gifts of listening, empowering, motivating, and coaching people to feel better about themselves, he helps people find more true joy in their work. Andrew's experiences have enabled him to evolve into a "purpose coach," helping people find success with fulfillment.

We can have success with fulfillment if our work is on purpose. As Norman Vincent Peale said, "Do your job naturally because you like it and success will take care of itself."

Our work takes up the largest chunk of our waking hours each week. To a large degree, it determines our quality of life depending on the location of the work and the amount of money earned. Where we live, who we become friends with, and what opportunities come our way are influenced by the work we do.

When the work we do is a mismatch with what we need and enjoy in basic ways, the mental and physical costs can be high. Problems in performance can result. Advancement is not as likely, and personal frustration and stress can be wearing.

Work can be more than just a job. It can be a source of "daily meaning *and* daily bread." The time taken to identify elements of purposeful work is well invested.

CHAPTER 11

A WORKING ON PURPOSE QUESTIONNAIRE

Purpose and laughter are the twins that must not separate.
Each is empty without the other.

—ROBERT K. GREENLEAF

The question arises, "How can I find purpose in the 'real work world'?" Many people argue against the practicality of finding purposeful work. Rarely, however, does anyone argue against the idea as such.

Some people detect their purpose very early; some late. Some purposes are work-related and some are spiritual or family- or community-driven. But the power of purpose always implies a relationship between a higher purpose and a higher power. We all differ as to what we are willing to commit ourselves to and as to what will stir up our deepest motives.

There appears to be a gap between supply and demand of a most central thing—meaningful work—work that fully engages our talents in something we believe in. One major reason is that we don't really expect work to give us much joy. I have observed at least four separate levels of work expectations:

- The first level is "it's just a job; any job is okay as long as the money is good and we can do our thing after work."

- The second level is that of a permanent job. At this level, "our work has to be regular; we need benefits, vacations, and . . . security."

- A third level is that of profession or trade. Rather than thinking only of money and security, "We want substance in our work. We want to grow our talents and be challenged." At this level, we are still profoundly concerned with money but we are also attached to the profession, or work, itself.

- A fourth level is that of vocation or calling. At this level, we realize that work is related to money but that work is also a path to use our gifts to make a difference doing something we believe needs doing in this world. We begin to consider the meaning that work can bring and the opportunity it allows us to follow a calling yet still have a marketable, income-producing involvement in the world.

Bringing meaning to our work starts with solitude and contemplation. We find it from the inside out. We sense that there is something unique and special that we can contribute and that the kind of work we do should relate to these contributions.

Take a moment to assess your working on purpose tendencies. What are the signs in your work that indicate "Yes, my work is on purpose"? What are the signs that indicate "No, my work isn't as joyful and fulfilling as I might wish"? Think of this questionnaire as you would think of taking a periodic physical examination.

A Working On Purpose Questionnaire	Yes	No
1. Do I wake up most Mondays feeling energized to go to work?	_____	_____
2. Do I have deep energy—feel a personal calling—for my work?	_____	_____
3. Am I clear about how I measure my success as a person?	_____	_____
4. Do I use my gifts to add real value to people's lives?	_____	_____
5. Do I work with people who honor the values I value?	_____	_____
6. Can I speak my truth in my work?	_____	_____
7. Am I experiencing true joy in my work?	_____	_____
8. Am I making a living doing what I most love to do?	_____	_____
9. Can I speak my purpose in one clear sentence?	_____	_____
10. Do I go to sleep most nights feeling "this was a well-lived day"?	_____	_____

Total "Yes" Responses = _____

Check either yes or no according to how you feel about each question today.

The total number of "Yes" responses on the Questionnaire provides a general idea of your power of purpose at work. If you have many "Yes" responses, you're obviously intent on making a difference through your work. You probably have a sense of purpose or direction, but you might consider further clarifying your gifts, passions, and values.

Eric Utne speaks with the confidence of someone who has heard it all before. Yet, at the same time, his words carry the caution of someone who has been carefully scrutinized by the media. The founder of both *New Age Journal* and *Utne Reader*, Eric's purpose for the latter was to "help the world become a little greener and a little kinder."

That is still his mission today. But today he's on a quest to become a little greener and a little kinder himself. He says his purpose is to "find and follow my heart." Beginning several years ago, Eric embarked on a journey to discover a more soulful approach to life. After meeting many of the world's notable shamans, mystics, and gurus, he felt it was time to find his own path. His path today has less to do with understanding and more to do with trust based on his own heart and wisdom, rather than on his accumulated knowledge.

Through many avenues, Eric is finding his heart through feeling his pain. He says with great joy, "I'm finally feeling." His work has been, in many ways, a search for a practice or a path that will help him work on his own purpose. Eric's ability to see the big picture, his need to know, and his commitment to social change often caused him to take himself a bit too seriously.

So, Eric took a one-year sabbatical from the *Utne Reader*. Upon turning 50, he felt pulled to spend more time at home and more time with his wife Nina. He felt that the very character traits that helped build the business were now in the way of growing, both in the business and in his marriage. "What's ripping my heart apart these days," he says, "is my transition from owner to chairman, from knowing to feeling, from doing to being."

Through a 12-day "vision fast" in the high desert of Death Valley, Eric slept and reflected alone for 4 days and 4 nights. He recalls, "There was a new stirring of energy within me. I realized that my life is now more about relationships and energy and less about work." He radiated a genuine warmth as he recalled the details of his experience.

The tiger has become Eric's symbol for change. He is involved in a small business venture selling Tibetan tiger rugs. In the Tibetan tantra tradition, the tiger represents the possibility of "becoming one with it and transformed by it." Eric says the tiger reminds me "to become one with my wild nature." He claims that the tiger comes to him in his dreams these days and appears in many ways in his life, reminding him to pay attention to his own wild nature and to work on purpose.

Not everyone has a work purpose. Many of us haven't even thought about our purpose. Others have several purposes. Some people feel they are led to a purpose through a spiritual experience. Others are having a crisis of purpose. Some of us have lost our purpose and are looking for a new one. Many of us fell into ours through someone else or by a strange coincidence, an unexpected event. Whatever our situation, the Working on Purpose Questionnaire is designed to help us reflect about working on purpose because when we're "on purpose," we have more deep energy and true joy in our lives.

CHAPTER 12

ESPRIT DE CORE™*

Spirituality is like the flu. Some get it; some don't

—MARILYN MASON

It's no revelation that many leaders are overwhelmed with change. They are being challenged today from every direction. Why do some leaders prosper whereas others don't?

We can speculate at length how some falter or fail due to failure to innovate, to anticipate market needs, or to grow. The real difference between success and failure today, however, can be traced directly to how well leaders inspire the hearts and discretionary energies of their followers. The one sure test of leadership is whether the leader has any true followers.

What does it take to inspire followers today? What does it take to rally people around a common purpose? It takes self-leadership. The difference between the success or the failure of leaders and

---

*Esprit de Core *is a trademark of The Inventure Group, of which Richard Leider is a partner.*

followers alike, today, can be traced to how successfully they lead themselves.

Doug Lennick is a self-led executive vice president of a large financial services company. For Doug, work is a natural expression of who he is, and it is a joyful experience. He says, "I'm clear that my work has to be a reflection of my heart and soul." He leads by trusting his inner voice.

Many people in Doug's organization claim that he is the soul of the company and one of the main reasons they are drawn to work there. One vice president states, "Doug is authentic—who he is at work, and who he thinks he is, are the same."

Doug reflects, "I love this company because I have the opportunity to pursue my passion of helping people grow. The main reason I continue to work here is for the opportunity to advance varying causes of human development. I have the heart of a social worker and the mind of a capitalist!"

"This job allows me to live the great American Dream to help others and to enjoy personal prosperity as a result, and to ultimately help our clients." Doug's purpose is "to help himself and others achieve the greatest potential for goodness."

Purpose defines the character of a leader. It defines a leader's motivations, boundaries and integrity. A sense of purpose accompanies greatness in anything and is largely responsible for the unity and courage found in high-performing teams.

My own organization, The Inventure Group, takes its purpose seriously. What moves us as a team is our challenge "to ignite the essence of growth and discovery in individuals, teams, and organizations." This simple statement describes the heart and soul of why we exist as an organization.

Our purpose is so natural and timeless, so basic and overarching, so individual and also universal that we use the words *Esprit de*

Core to describe it. *Esprit de Core* is the heart of purpose—spirit of the core. *Esprit de Core* means that spirit and energy come from the inside out.

Each Inventure Group employee is there to ignite the spirit of growth and discovery within themselves as well as in their clients. All team members try to express their own gifts on things that move them. Senior Partner Steve Buchholz came via a major training company, where he was an executive responsible for program design. In that organization, Steve reflects, "We lost our energy and meaning. I couldn't find the meaning in my own work. Form was being emphasized over essence."

Steve left to find a place where he could fully represent the human aspect of change. Through his own work experiences, he was motivated to make organizations more accountable to the human side of change. Today, Steve is an internationally known consultant on change. His purpose, "to help people make quality choices about their work and their lives" drives his work passion. He enjoys using his gifts as a program designer and coach to develop the organization's workshop facilitators, like Mike Mayberry.

Mike came to The Inventure Group from the coaching field, where he was a high school and college basketball coach with a winning reputation. Starting his coaching career at Muleshoe, Texas, he thrived on coaching under adversity. His teams throughout his career were known for their character—consistently overcoming adversity and winning sportsmanship awards in spite of their records.

At one point, however, his junior college basketball team was ranked number 2 in the nation, but his sportsmanship theme had been sacrificed to get there. His team, like Steve's prior organization, was all form and no essence. The game, for Mike, was empty. He recalls, "It just didn't have the soul I was after. We would sell out the coliseum, but I wasn't making a difference. The players just wanted to play in the National Basketball Association and I was the guy who could help them get there. It just didn't have the spirit I was after anymore."

Leaving coaching, Mike tried several things, including successfully managing a college bookstore. But he was hungry for a new game, a new arena to coach in. Attending an Inventure Group seminar, he decided his new mission was to be a life-planning coach. Today, as a coach to corporate leaders and teams, Mike's purpose is "to fully live in the present moment, learning and growing, coaching myself and others to live a life of no regrets."

Mike's learning curve was about as steep as John Busacker's. As the director of business development for The Inventure Group, John shifted gears after 13 years as a manager and salesman in the financial services industry.

Many of John's friends, family, and former colleagues comment on how relaxed and at ease he seems these days. Although working harder and spending more hours than ever with work, John feels a natural ease or flow to doing work that he is passionate about. He says, "I get up with a sense of energy I never dreamed was possible. I have a great opportunity to be of service to people in a deeper way." John clarified that his purpose is "to call greatness out of people."

Both John and Mike truly have the gift of "igniting the essence of growth and discovery" in their clients. And both have discovered, with Noel Coward, that "work is more fun than fun." They are self-directed "inventurers" whose lives inspire others.

Barb Hoese is also an inventurer who describes herself as a person who was "born old and is growing young." Her very serious nature when she was young led to her academic success and high school valedictory address where she wisely, beyond her years, advised her classmates that "some people make things happen; some people watch things happen; and some people don't know anything happened!"

The serious journey to her purpose continued in college where she increasingly felt passionate about helping people understand that they have to "make things happen" for themselves. In addition, through exposure to a wide variety of new people and ideas, she started growing younger by taking her work seriously, not herself.

Today, as vice president of operations for The Inventure Group, the journey continues in earnest as Barb lives her purpose of "helping people understand the power of choices in their lives." In her continuing quest to "grow young," Barb sees work more like play— the best kind, with clear rules, competent players, and with purpose and laughter. And best of all is the joy that comes from "making things happen."

Lisa Capistrant has also been living in the question of purpose since college. She grew up in a family that encouraged her to have fun, try anything once, but not to grow up too fast! A fan of theater and movies, she adopted the quote uttered by Rosalind Russell in *Auntie Mame*—"Life is a banquet, and most of you poor suckers are starving to death"—as her life theme.

Lisa says her work environment legitimizes her joy in helping clients appreciate life as a banquet. As the Inventure Group's information coordinator, she's the first contact for many people, nurturing relationships along from the very beginning and helping determine how they can ignite the essence of growth and discovery.

Lisa's purpose, "to be a master gardener, nurturing everything I come into contact with," aligns nicely with her life and work. Exploring and appreciating as much of God's world as possible, she talks to cats, plants, and all sentient beings. She seeks to have fun at life's banquet and provide nurturing to The Inventure Group's clients.

Cara Connelly's purpose also has to do with nurturing. As client services manager, Cara's purpose is "to help people develop, nurture and have positive relationships." She says, "I'm totally passionate about positive relationships and I'm intense when I don't see it happening."

When Cara was a child, she wanted more than anything for everybody to get along. She could, at a very young age, sense when people were not connecting. Now, when she meets people, she's immediately curious about what it is that defines a healthy relationship for them. Cara is moved by relationships. She believes that people must create their relationships, not be created by them.

The Inventure Group has been a catalyst for naming and living Cara's purpose. She says, "We as a company don't think people should settle for less than purposeful work and purposeful relationships. All our programs focus on purpose and relationships." Cara is a catalyst for deep, positive, and "courageous conversations" with staff and clients alike. Cara embodies the old adage, "As the flower unfolds, the bees come uninvited." People are naturally attracted to her care and openness.

Working as part of The Inventure Group team has deepened my belief that purpose is the most important criteria we as individuals have for choosing what to do with our lives. Purpose is the conscious choice of applying our gifts to teams and in organizations that move us—in which we believe. Although diverse in age and individual purpose, our team believes we can truly ignite the essence of growth and discovery in our clients. We clearly feel the connection between spirit and work.

Many teams, organizations, and leaders are rediscovering the connection between spirit and work. Warren Malkerson, vice president and general manager of a large sporting goods catalogue company, has felt this connection through his whole life but didn't understand it until he was in his late thirties. As a business leader, he relates, "I always got criticized for caring too much about people. I felt a struggle being on the 'soft side,' like the ugly duckling."

One day he realized he was, in fact, not the ugly duckling, but a swan; that caring for people was not only worthwhile but also productive. Wherever he worked, it's always been said, "his people always seem to be the happier, more creative folks in the organization."

Warren believes there's a swan in every one of us. His purpose is "to help others discover their potential—the swan inside." He feels that every human is struggling to unlock his or her potential. He helps people to stretch outside the box, to see that the world is not that scary.

Warren views every mistake as a learning experience. He considers his leadership to be effective when his employees say, "I've never worked so hard and learned so much. He makes me learn!" He pledges to people when he hires them that they'll always be able to answer "yes" to the question, "Was this one of your best learning experiences?"

Like one of his heroes, the late quality guru Edward Deming, Warren believes, "I don't have to convert everybody! I'm not a missionary. I'm not here to help those who don't want to be helped. But my purpose is to help those who want to learn on purpose!"

Leaders like Warren, who clearly ask and struggle to answer questions of purpose, discover that new products, services, and ways of doing business often evolve and that the personal meaning people wish to have in their work is satisfied.

A primary role of 21st-century leadership is to answer the question many followers are asking today: "Why should I follow you?" Today, purposeful leaders understand that all change is self-change; we really can't compel people to do anything. We can only encourage them to want to do things. They understand that today, real commitment and discretionary energy come through *Esprit de Core*.

During more than 20 years as a career coach to many leaders, I have been continually impressed with the hunger that great leaders have for some purpose higher than just personal career and financial success. They want to know clearly what they are leading for.

We are hungry today for leaders who are authentic sources of *Esprit de Core*. We hunger for leaders who guide from the inside out and who lead with integrity. Integrity results from each of our acts making a statement as to our purpose. Purpose is something leaders and organizations live every day. It is what they do rather than what they say.

Purpose cannot be created by simply writing words on a page. It is embodied in a leader's calendar and checkbook—the way a leader spends his or her time and money (resources). It grows out of the deepest part of a leader's character and convictions.

Leading on purpose means keeping the small promises we make to ourselves and to others. The concept of integrity is made clear by thinking about our friends who honestly keep their small promises and by comparing them to friends who don't. When we're with friends who "walk their talk," we have a high level of trust that their promises will be kept. Less integrated friends make promises or commitments that are vague, unclear, or not kept. Though they may intend to live up to their word, their words don't compare to their actions. We naturally compare what leaders say their purpose is with what they do; we compare what they say with their actions.

Leaders today have to come to terms with spirit in the workplace. Spirituality is an aspect of our work lives that is not discussible in many organizations. Yet why do so many people in leadership positions go to churches, mosques, and temples or otherwise ponder the meaning of the circumstances they find themselves in? What goes on in their leadership minds as they ponder the great questions: "Who am I?" "What am I meant to do here?" "What am I trying to do with my life?"

Leaders empowered by a sense of purpose are enthusiastic about the possibility their leadership holds for creating *Esprit de Core* in the workplace. The original Greek word for enthusiasm meant "to be filled with God." When we are "filled with God" we tend to lead on purpose. People today desperately need leaders who lead with spirit, whatever the spiritual tradition of their inspiration.

PART IV

PATHS TO PURPOSE

CHAPTER 13

ARE YOU LIVING FROM THE INSIDE OUT?

We can discover this meaning in life in three different ways:
(1) by doing a deed; (2) by experiencing a value; and (3) by suffering.

—VIKTOR FRANKL

Where do you start? How do you decide where to commit yourself? How do you make your living work?

Our work is the purpose we live by transformed into action. If we open our eyes to the world around us, we often notice the endless "work" that calls for our energies and talents.

- Which part of the newspaper, or issues, do you read about regularly?

- Which TV specials are you drawn to watch?

- Which parts of your organization's strategic plans interest you?

- What speeches or presentations have moved you?

- Which "on purpose" leaders inspire you?

- Which special-interest newsletters do you subscribe to?

- What needs of your church, synagogue, temple, or spiritual organization interest you?

- What part of your political party's platform moves you?

For most of us, the community in which we live is rich with possibilities for gaining greater meaning and purpose. To discover our calling, we need to live from the inside out—see the potential issues that move us.

Viktor Frankl points to three ways to make a living work: "We can discover this meaning in life in three different ways: by doing a deed; by experiencing a value; and by suffering."

"DOING A DEED"

One way to start is to "discover" what's needed and wanted, and then produce it—right where we are—in our current work, family, spiritual organization, or community.

John Horan-Kates feels a major need today is to promote "balanced living." As a founder and executive director of The White River Institute in Vail, Colorado, John's purpose is to "promote and facilitate balanced living, by living it myself, and by bringing people to the mountains for healthful, educational, and recreational programs." The White River Institute researches, designs, and delivers programs for balanced living. Through the institute, John wants to help people "take the cure" in the mountains where they can relax, reacquaint, and re-create. He wants to give substance to the expression "recreation with a purpose."

John's combined passions for family, the mountains, and education, together with his gifts as an idea developer, have given birth to the White River Institute. Through the institute, John is playing a key part in building the "balanced living" world he wants to live in.

Visible achievement and accomplishment of deeds—especially those we have had something to say about creating—are important. These can seem trivial to an outsider, but they are important from a personal perspective. For deeds to have a real impact at a personal level, we must own the issue in a personally committed way. Claiming some deed set by others or expected of us is not nearly as satisfying. This, however, does not mean that whatever deed we select needs to be large or even visible to others. It is "do-gooders," who need to keep score of their virtues. "Keeping score" may actually reduce our sense of contentment as we clearly see how our commitment is driven by external (or ego) influences.

"EXPERIENCING A VALUE"

Our core values guide our behavior. If identified and clear to us, a superordinate value can serve as a source of purpose. The reverse is also true. When circumstances or our own weaknesses lead us to act counter to our core values, we feel poorly about ourselves and we can become depressed.

Purpose calls us to be the unique individuals that we are. Bernie Saunders, like each of us, is one of a kind. He chose his life's work as a writer, trainer, and learning consultant on the basis of his joy for learning. On the path to discovering his calling, first he had to go through the struggle of "getting out from under the desk."

In first grade during the first month of school, Bernie explains how he hid under his teacher's desk, not wanting to come out. He relates his fear: "I had no power and control in that room. I was overwhelmed that what was happening inside the classroom had absolutely nothing to do with what was going on outside where I did have control. I felt stupid, inadequate, and did not fit socially or in sports."

Bernie carried that "under the desk" feeling all the way through the Peace Corps and graduate school. Finally, after graduate school, he discovered the joy of learning, the joy in being passionate about discovery. He discovered it "was safe for little Bernie to come out from under the desk."

His passion for discovery is expressed in his purpose today: "To create environments and spaces for people to tap the joy of natural learning." As an author, consultant, and workshop leader, he calls us to be our unique selves when he says, "Life is art! Your obligation is to discover your form of art."

Daring to be ourselves—our own special design—is a personal and difficult issue because it involves solitude and contemplation, which are unnatural activities for many people. And it is not something another person can do for us, because reflection is a discovery process.

"SUFFERING"

There are crises that significantly reduce the quality of life for most of us. These situations are so devastating that our entire sense of meaning may slip, leaving us shaken or enraged. At such times, feelings of shock and of being in limbo are not uncommon. When we cope effectively, a purpose may actually be found or strengthened or made clearer. We often learn more about who we really are under conditions of "suffering." The following are examples of triggering events, which cause us to reassess our purpose: death of loved one, divorce, marital separation, major illness or disability, loss of work, major geographic move, retirement, major financial gain or loss.

These kinds of events cause most of us, at least temporarily, to ask the big questions: "Who am I?" "What am I meant to do here?" "What am I trying to do with my life?" Our life trajectory and the basic sense of who we are often are disrupted, and we are reawakened the purpose and meaning we need so much.

Tucked away just outside the town of Osceola, Wisconsin, is a place every person should know about. The Aveda Spa is synonymous with living from the inside out. And Nasreen Koaser embodies the mission of the Aveda Corporation: "to promote and support continuous learning as a foundation for success and well-being." Consistent with Aveda's philosophy, Nasreen strives to bring out the "pure essence" in her clients. A hair stylist, or "image crafter" as her card reads, Nasreen brings such pure love and healing touch to her work that people come from all distances to fill up her calendar months in advance. In our busy, fast-paced, over-scheduled world, Nasreen awaits her clients with hot tea, a kind word, healing touch, and an open heart.

She was invited to work at the Aveda Spa by its founder, Horst Rechelbacher. He saw the spiritual contribution she could make there. Arriving at Aveda five years ago from her native India, Nasreen was cut off from everything—family, friends, food, and spiritual customs. The change caused her to go deep inside to discover the true nature of herself and her work. She strives to make people happy by helping them feel good about themselves. She says, "I love my work because I love my clients. Every day God gives me the opportunity to bring out the pure essence in my clients. That is my purpose and I am grateful for work that allows me to use my gifts in this way."

By living from the inside out, we begin to consider the possibility of new roles and purposes. In the early stages, the process is one of a grasping search for new external sources of pleasure to fill the void produced by the loss. But with time, the pain subsides and gradually gives way to hope about the future—a new vision of ourselves. Our priorities shift to growing in new ways. As we adapt to the change and normalize our lives, we feel empowered with new confidence and competence. And, we feel the deep joy of living from the inside out.

CHAPTER 14

DISCOVER YOUR GIFTS

Most of us go to our graves with our music still inside us.

—OLIVER WENDELL HOLMES

What are my gifts? How can I best give my gifts to something in which I believe—a value, product, person, service, ideal, problem, or organization? The power in purpose means discovering our gifts— those that we're already aware of and are motivated to master and those that are emerging that we would like to try or explore. Although talents are a part of everyday vocabulary, few people try to state clearly what their natural gifts are. The power behind our purpose is knowing and using our natural gifts.

We each possess gifts and valuable talents. This fundamental assumption has proved true for everyone whom I have coached over the past 20 years. Everyone is gifted in some way. Many of us might deny that this is the case simply because we have never focused on our strengths; rather, we have focused on our weaknesses.

We all have natural abilities and inclinations and find that certain things come easily to us. We may perform a talent so effortlessly that we forget we have it. This is a "gift." We might not have had to pay the price to buy this gift because it came so easily; we were born with it! We may never even have had to practice it extensively.

The Puritan ethic has convinced many of us that anything requiring hard work is valuable and anything that comes easily and does not require hard work is worth less. About our gifts we often think, "This comes easily, so it must be easy for everyone." We underestimate its worth. Actually, our gifts are our most powerful talents of all. And to be fulfilled in our work, we must discover and express them.

Caroline Otis has been a writer by trade for more than 20 years. Her work has allowed her to use and develop important gifts, and its freedom has allowed her to work in the home she loves and schedule her days around the needs of the people she loves. Over the years, many questioning friends have asked, "Why are you so happy all the time?" Caroline's answer has been that "my life is a blend of work, momness, community involvement, physical expression, and singing in the choir."

Now, however, as her children leave for college, it's clear that parenting has been her most purposeful work. This realization—that helping young people move toward the future with confidence and a sense of joy—has moved Caroline to consider working with other adolescents to help them get off to a flying start.

Caroline says her purpose today is "to help young people to discover their purpose, to identify and develop their strengths and passions, and to tear into the world of work with energy and joy."

She grew up believing that if she couldn't be the best at something, why bother to try? When she hit 40, however, it became clear to her that "anything worth doing is worth doing badly." She learned more from trying something new—no matter how bad at it she was—than doing what she was already good at.

So Caroline joined a gospel choir—not because she was good at singing but because she loved to sing, especially gospel music. The choir has been a great lesson, because gospel singing is about emptying yourself out so the spirit can flow into you and out of you. It isn't about performing well but about giving what you've got.

In that gospel spirit—and because she loves movies—she took a sabbatical after her children left home to work on the crew of *Lone Star*, the film by writer, director, editor John Sayles, who is also a novelist. She claims, "I worked on the film as a cable puller in the sound department—and I was a pretty inept cable puller, at that!" But she learned a lot about filmmaking and about herself.

When Caroline attended the film's preview at the South by Southwest Film Festival, she was struck by a question from the audience. A man asked John Sayles if he ever got discouraged and thought about not being a writer and filmmaker anymore. And John replied that he doesn't think of himself as a writer. He doesn't define himself as a filmmaker. He just gets passionate about stories, he said, and he loves to find the best ways to tell those stories—be it by the written word or film. For John, his purpose is anchored solidly in finding and telling the stories that move him.

For Caroline, the quantum leap now is to find work that she loves and give herself to it—"dip her oar in the river and paddle hard!" And if one venture doesn't work out, the river will reveal another interesting bend, just as long as she keeps paddling. Her purpose and passion is to help adolescents, like her own children, "get off to a flying start in life."

Some researchers say that we have numerous talents and ways of experiencing our innate intelligence. Discovering our unique talents is the power that drives purpose. Based on the research of Howard Gardner, a Harvard University educator, there are eight core categories that summarize the talents we each have. The theory of "multiple intelligences" was first attributed to Gardner in 1983. In his book *Frames of Mind*, he reported on his original studies, which concluded that all people have at least seven intelligences. He recently added an eighth. How do you see yourself fitting into these eight areas? Which areas are you strongest in? Weakest in?

1. *Linguistic*—Do you like word games, puns, rhymes, or tongue twisters? Do you use words persuasively and correctly? If you are attracted to this area, then language—reading, writing, and speaking are your natural talents. You are able to write clearly and can instruct or communicate through the spoken word.

2. *Logical*—Do you use numbers effectively? Do you like facts, figures, or balancing your checkbook? If you are attracted to this area, then numbers and logic—reasoning, critical thinking, and mathematical problem solving—are your natural talents. You are able to see how things react by taking a rational, logical approach to life.

3. *Spatial*—Do you think visually? Do you have a vivid imagination or perceive colors, textures, and shapes accurately? If you are attracted to this area, then thinking in pictures and images using shapes and colors to envision the world around you are your natural talents. You are able to visualize, draw, paint, or sketch your ideas and are easily oriented to three-dimensional spaces.

4. *Musical*—Do you like humming tunes, making them up, or singing along with the radio? Do you appreciate and understand rhythm? If you are attracted to this area, then rhythms and melodies—singing in tune, keeping time to rhythms, and having an ear for music—are your natural abilities. You are

able to listen to and discern different selections of musical pieces and appreciate compositions of all kinds.

5. *Kinesthetic*—Do you like to exercise, play sports, dance, or work with your hands? Do you move your body effectively? If you are attracted to this area, then handling objects, demonstrating athletic prowess or hands-on problem solving are your natural abilities. You are able to put things together, build models, sculpt, dance, and enjoy physical activities of all kinds.

6. *Interpersonal*—Do you like to tune into the feelings of others? Do you relate successfully with others including teamwork? If you are attracted to this area, then tuning into the needs, feelings and desires of others—understanding and working with others—are your natural abilities. You are able to see the world from another's perspective and connect effectively with people in the world around you.

7. *Intrapersonal*—Do you like to meditate or ponder the imponderables? Do you enjoy solitude and reflection? If you are attracted to this area, then being self-directed—aware of the inner self and inner feelings—are your natural abilities. You are able to spend time alone to reflect on the world around you in an independent, self-disciplined, and self-motivated way.

8. *Naturalistic*—Do you like to classify and analyze how things fit together? If you are attracted to this area, then sensing, understanding, and systematically classifying the natural world—the environment—are your natural abilities. You have an intuitive sense of how things fit together and are able to distinguish interrelationships in the world.

Looking at talents with Gardner's framework expands the possibilities for discovering our gifts. It enables us to place a greater value on the broad range of our talents and helps us see our differences as strengths. Our ability to discover and embrace our unique gifts establishes the power behind our purpose.

If you wish to spend the time and energy to discover or confirm your talents in depth, you might consider reading one of the resource books in the bibliography with good talent sections. If you're confused as to what your gifts are, you can ask your spouse, a friend, a colleague, a supervisor, or someone who knows you very well to help you clarify and focus on your strengths.

The idea that we should find joy in our work is one that many people both accept and question. Yet it seems to make sense that we do best at that which we enjoy most. There's always the idea that work is something to be tolerated and leisure is something to be enjoyed. Yet, work consumes the most significant number of our waking hours. When we consider that about 60% of our life's time is spent working, it might seem to be good common sense to discover and use our most enjoyed gifts. We can refuse to go to our graves, as Oliver Wendell Holmes observed, "with our music still inside us."

Early in life, we learn to feel that some talents are more valuable to society than others are. Thus, we often don't acknowledge our gifts because we believe, "How could I make a living doing that?" or "What economic value could that gift possibly have?"

Knowing ourselves—what we do well and enjoy doing—is important not only for making career decisions but also for empowering our purpose. Any good work decision should be based on our answer to the question, "Is this work likely to be a good match for my most enjoyed gifts?"

CHAPTER 15

DISCOVER WHAT MOVES YOU

I have a dream ...

—MARTIN LUTHER KING

Now that you have considered your gifts—the power—where do you apply them? To what passion? An important next step is to discover what moves you. This is the hardest part for many of us because we believe the old adage, "Anything worth doing is worth doing well." Most of the emphasis has mistakenly been put on the "worth doing well." The real question, however, is "what's worth doing?"—a much neglected question for many of us.

When you have a good idea of what your gifts are and what moves you, you have the power of purpose. Life and work decisions based on both gifts and passion produce energy, flow, and aliveness.

When I wrote an earlier version of this book, I worked at a small antique desk in my 100-year-old hand-hewn immigrant log cabin in the northwoods of Wisconsin. I was surrounded by books on the topic, so absorbed in my task I sometimes felt I was in an altered state of consciousness. I often lost track of time as idea after idea popped into my mind from some deep well of sources. According to University of Chicago psychologist Mihalyi Csikszentmihalyi, I was in "flow"—so passionate about my topic that I lost touch with time.

In his book *Flow: The Psychology of Optimal Experience*, Csikszentmihalyi believes we come closest to total fulfillment when in the flow state. He has concluded from his research that a passionate drive to solve problems and meet challenges causes us to derive pleasure from performing at our peak. By finding ourselves, our passions, we lose ourselves in time.

To consider potential opportunities where we can plug in our gifts, we must "tap into the flow state," to think of what needs move us in our work organization, our family, our community, or society in general and to examine those problems, issues, or concerns that we feel passionate about. What are the needs of people, of your family, neighborhood, community, business, spiritual organization, the world? What needs doing? What issues do you truly feel "someone oughta do something about"?

To stimulate your thinking, ask yourself these questions:

- If you were asked to create a TV special about something that moves you, what would it be about?

- What magazines intrigue you most at a newsstand? What sections or articles capture your attention?

- If you started a business or organization in order to solve a need, what would it be?

- What issue would you like to see someone write a best-selling book about?

- What subjects would you like to learn about? Go back to school for? Study under a master in?

- In the past years, what were your favorite causes? What interests do they reflect?

- Who are the people you find yourself voluntarily getting together with, again and again, for deeper discussions? What are your deepest conversations about?

- How would you use a gift of a million dollars if it had to be given away or designated for a cause, issue, or problem that moves you?

- Is there any need or problem you believe in so strongly you'd love to work at it full time if you were paid well to do it?

Matthew Fox writes that "a spirituality of work is about bringing life and livelihood back together again. And spirit with them." He claims, "Spirit means life, and both life and livelihood are about living in depth, living with meaning, purpose, joy, and a sense of contributing to the greater community." Does this statement from Fox name your experience of work?

Sally Humphries Leider says, "I've always felt natural doing what I'm doing. I love to teach children, to bring out their essence, their spirit." Throughout her life, Sally has immediately connected with children as her natural learning partners. Ever since she was in the third grade, Sally was in awe of teachers. She says, "My fantasy was to be able to sit on the ground outdoors with my second-grade teacher and just talk."

When Sally started her teaching career in the city, she missed the out-of-doors most of all. Having grown up on a river in nature, she says, "I was given the gift of place—the gift of growing up in a place which was rich with the sounds, sights, and smells of nature. I took place for granted until my parents died and I couldn't go back to the river anymore." She tried to find the same feeling in other places but couldn't find it.

Sally's parents were environmentally active, willing to fight, lobby, and educate people about preserving the natural river valley they lived in. Sally carries on their battle. As a professional environmental educator, Sally says her purpose is "to instill the love of the natural world in children." She feels a legacy to continue the hard work her parents left her of maintaining the natural harmony in nature. Her purpose moves her to teach kids to maintain that balance or to bring that balance back. Her parents gave her the place, growing up, to love nature and notice things in nature. They taught her what's worth saving and preserving and working for.

Sally's deep passion is ecology—harmony with nature, not dominance over nature. She believes in the intrinsic value of all nature, rather than the natural environment as a resource for human exploitation. She believes that "biodiversity, the total variety of life on earth, is collapsing at mind-boggling rates. The accelerating loss of plant and animal species is occurring all over the planet."

To stop the losses, Sally believes that a critical aspect of education is for children to experience nature directly. She says, "To the extent that children can discover for themselves a special connection with the natural world, they will be potentially motivated to take action to preserve the Earth's species and ecosystems. That's my mission, to give them that experience."

At the end of *Flow*, Csikszentmihalyi offers a prescription for the power of purpose. He says we can transform our whole life into a unified flow experience by approaching our activities in a certain way, by pursuing what he calls a "life theme." Whatever our passion, whether it be educating children, raising happy children, or finding a cure for AIDS, "as long as it provides clear objectives, clear rules for action, and a way to concentrate and become involved, any goal can serve to give meaning to a person's life."

Let's be systematic about this and run through a list of possible new passions for you to consider. Review the following "life themes." Discover what moves you.

CHALLENGED POPULATIONS

Blind and Visually Impaired

Veterans

Deaf and Hearing Impaired

Elderly/Aging

Special Education

Barrier-Free Access

Special Olympics

Speech Disorders

Poor/Fixed Incomes

Learning Disabled

Medical System Advocacy

Legal and Welfare Rights

Homebound Services

Criminal Justice

Kinship Programs/Big Brothers & Sisters, Etc.

Other?

HEALTH CARE

Hospices/Health Care Facilities

Smoking, Alcohol, Drug Education

Mental Health

First Aid and Safety

Chemical Dependency

Wellness

Fitness

Healing

Nutrition

Abortion

Emergency Food and Clothing

Eating Disorders

Medical Research

Disease (cancer, heart, blood, etc.)

AIDS

Other?

COMMUNITY

Disaster Relief

Educational Quality/Literacy

Animal Services/Rights

Housing/Neighborhood Improvement

Consumer Information/ Complaints

Arts/Culture

Political Change/Voter Registration

Civil Rights/Racism

Immigration/Refugee Resettlement

Hunger

Other?

WOMEN/MEN/CHILDREN/FAMILY

Homemaker Services

Family Planning

Day Care

Employment of Youth

Foster Care

Money Management

Abuse (physical, sexual, other)

Education of the Gifted

Adoption

Education of Parents

Single Parenting

Men's Organizations

Women's Organizations

Other?

SPIRITUALITY

Religious Service Organizations

Mission Work

Family-life Education

Ecumenical Movement

Social Action Groups

Spiritual Direction

Spiritual Study, Renewal, Practices

Youth Outreach

Religious Education

Crisis Intervention

Other?

WORK
Employment (older worker, youth, etc.)
Productivity
Quality of Work Life
Financial Counseling
Working Women
Working Mothers
Life Balance
Equal Employment
Retirement
Human Relations
Other?

ENVIRONMENT
Energy Alternatives
Pollution
Urban/Renewal
Recycling
Agriculture
Recreation (national parks, wild rivers)
Biodiversity/Preservation of Nature
Mass Transit
Population
Nuclear Waste
Water Quality
Other?

All the people in this book who discovered what moved them had to overcome their self-imposed doubts and obstacles to getting started. The following are three common obstacles to our passionately moving ahead toward our purpose. As you read each one, ask yourself, "Do I believe this?"

OBSTACLE 1: TO HAVE PURPOSE MEANS I MUST DO SOMETHING COMPLETELY ORIGINAL.

Can you think of anything that is totally new? Almost every idea or thing created is an extension or synthesis of previous ideas. New scientific breakthroughs are built on existing fundamental truths. New breakthroughs are often the result of reorganizing and applying old ideas. Like runners in a relay race, we simply carry the baton another leg of the race. As we discover our purpose, we often accept the fact that at the heart of most new ideas is the borrowing, adding, combining, or modifying of old ones.

The paradox of purpose is that in order to address new solutions to problems we must first familiarize ourselves with the ideas of others. The ideas form a base for launching our own ideas. Gather as much information as you can (realizing that you'll never have enough). Make a decision. Get on with the business of working on purpose.

OBSTACLE 2: ONLY A FEW SPECIAL PEOPLE HAVE TRUE PURPOSE IN THEIR LIVES.

This is the most commonly rationalized of all myths. There is no denying that often we have relied on saints, sages and experts to solve many of our problems. History, however, is filled with great contributions made by people with virtually no expertise in the areas where they made their mark. Being a novice is often an asset because we aren't hemmed in by traditional ways of viewing a situation.

Purpose appears in proportion to the passion of the energies we expend, rather than to our degree of expertness. It's the passion to make a difference that counts most.

The "pop-in" theory of motivation would have us believe that creative ideas or new directions are flashes of brilliance that suddenly appear to a fortunate few. Purpose descends on the lucky recipient. If we believe that, nothing will happen for sure! Meaning comes to those who seek it. Any successful person can attest to the absurdity of "waiting" to be inspired. First we begin. Then the insights appear.

OBSTACLE 3: PURPOSE IS NICE, BUT IMPRACTICAL. I'M JUST TOO BUSY!

Many times we become so rutted in day-to-day survival activity that we lose sight of what we're doing, and our activity becomes a false end in itself rather than a means to an end. Henry David Thoreau put it bluntly: "It isn't enough to be busy. Ants are busy." The question we should ask ourselves is: "What are we busy about?"

"Gee, I'd love to get involved, but who's got the time? I have a spouse, job, children, and financial commitments. How on earth can you expect me to find the time?" Sound familiar? For most of us, time is indeed the scarce resource.

Waiting until we have the time is as futile as trying to save money by putting away what we don't happen to spend. The only way to commit time to purpose is to steal it from some other present activity. This is what the power of purpose is all about—aligning our energies around our true priorities.

At one time or another, most of us have experienced "flow"— the power *and* the purpose coming together in a task so challenging that we lose track of the world around us. In the book *Flow*, Mihaly Csikszentmihalyi has observed that almost everyone can experience flow by taking the following steps:

- Pick an activity, one that moves you.

- Raise the bar by challenging yourself to use your gifts to their highest level.

- Make sure your activity has clear goals and immediate feedback so you know how you're doing and you don't burn out from lack of real results.

- Screen out distractions, both external and internal, so you can achieve the total concentration that produces flow.

- Focus total attention on what you're doing so that your deepest energies are engaged.

CHAPTER 16

DISCOVER SOLITUDE

If you look up the word 'spirit' in the dictionary, you will find that it comes from the Latin spirare, *meaning 'to breathe.' . . . In the deepest sense, the breath itself is the ultimate gift of spirit.*

—JON KABAT-ZINN

It's often as we turn toward solitude that our calling becomes apparent. Periodically we need to give ourselves time to sit quietly and let our souls catch up with our bodies; time to listen to the still, small voice inside. How can we hear our calling if we do not create time to listen? Do you provide time in your life for solitude?

To reach in under the surface of things, we need to pay genuine attention to all that's there. Discovering a sense of purpose through the busy routines of work and home is not easy. Our daily routine often lacks a sense of "why?" Life sometimes appears to have no purpose, to serve no apparent ends.

Great is the need in our lives for deliberate reminders of the "why." Yet we create precious little time for regular reflection.

Through solitude and contemplation, we see beneath the surface. We know not with the mind but with the heart. Our intuitive side recognizes a power beyond the natural and rational and accepts the unknown on faith.

There are steps we can take to enhance our reflectiveness and consequently open our listening. Solitude often enhances our big picture perspective and taps our deep energy. When we get out of touch with our core, we lose our life energy. We gain back our energy and vitality by solitude—and by letting our reflective insights guide our day-to-day decisions.

At times we are receptive to solitude; at other times, we are not. At times crises drop into our lives and we are forced to reflect—to deal with the "Who am I?", "What am I here to do?" and "What am I trying to do with my life?" questions. At other times we don't sense the need at all. Our intuition rusts silently from lack of use.

A major element of reflection is to plan regular "solos"—times for solitude—to be quiet and not distracted by our busyness. The more regularly we take solos, the more we start unmasking illusions. Slowly we start discerning what parts of our busyness are expressions of our real purpose. Hearing a calling requires regular silence. Solitude is, for many of us, as tough as it is inevitable. A solo can help us see and appreciate our entire life pattern. Soloing is simply a process of sitting quietly and listening on a regular basis.

"How do I take a solo?"

First of all, sit down! In the morning, for instance, get up a little earlier, and before you get involved in anything, just sit quietly and take a few deep breaths. Then focus on your purpose. Picture yourself moving through the day on purpose. An architect first has an idea or a plan, then designs a building. An artist often has a similar inspiration. Think of your solo as time to create a blueprint for your day.

Some people are inclined to take a solo every day. Some are more inclined weekly or monthly to go to a quiet place to reflect. Others create solo time when they're driving long distances, walking, jogging, listening to music, praying, or meditating.

Ideally, we should not let a day pass without spending some solo time listening. Eventually we really start listening to our deepest selves. The solo is a practice to discover our deepest, most basic purpose in life.

Try this 10-minute solo exercise. Solitude and relaxation both play important roles in reflection. In a quiet, relaxed state, we find it easier to concentrate our attention in the direction we choose and to develop a much clearer perception of the events in our lives.

- Sit in a comfortable position. Consciously examine your physical tension and describe it to yourself in detail. Examine its intensity. Become as aware as you possibly can of the tension and related discomfort. Tighten up this area; then relax it. If you touch the tense area with your hand, you will feel the discomfort. Interesting areas to try are your jaw, back, neck, and eye muscles. Most people are tense in these areas without being fully aware of it.

- Close your eyes. Take several slow, deep breaths, breathing from your abdomen. Breathe in and out through your nose, taking breaths that are long and slow. Silently count "one" as you inhale and "two" as you exhale. Do this over and over again for several minutes. Concentrate on the numbers 1 and 2, saying them to yourself for each breathing cycle. The idea here is to clear your mind. Most of us feel controlled by thoughts that constantly pop into our minds. Visualize your thoughts as clouds floating toward you, floating freely into your mind, and then floating out of your mind again. Keep going back to counting your breaths. It will become easier as you practice.

- After you've enjoyed yourself in the quiet for several minutes, spend three to four minutes picturing your day happening ideally just as you want it. Why are you getting up this morning? What work calls forth your gifts? What moves you? Where do you see yourself working—what kind of environment? Don't worry if you don't actually see a place in your mind. Some people do, but others feel that they don't really see anything; they just have a feeling impression. That will do just fine.

- Keeping the picture in your mind, affirm silently to yourself, "My work is now flowing together around my gifts and passions." To affirm means to "make firm" that which you are picturing. If doubts or contradictory thoughts arise, don't resist them; just let them flow through your mind, and return to your images.

- Don't be in a big hurry to open your eyes. Before you do, suggest to yourself that you are getting more and more alert—that you will feel clear and calm when you return.

As you see, the solo process is relatively simple. Using it really effectively, however, requires consistent practice.

Al Fahden, author, inventor and creativity consultant, is focusing his quest to find a calling into which he can pour his immense creative gifts. He has a strong sense that his purpose today is to "be a doorway to the changing world," but he's not sure exactly what that means.

So, to discover which door to open, Al regularly uses a solo and questioning process, which he likens to a purpose Ouiji Board. He recently asked his "Ouiji coach" these questions:

Q: "Have I been on purpose?" A: "No!"

Q: "Is it a matter of focus?" A: "No!"

Q: "Is it about being a creative person?" A: "No!"

Q: "Is it about writing the screenplay I've always wanted to write?" A: "No!"

Q: "Should I stop everything I'm doing?" A: "No!"

Q: "Should I refocus something I'm already doing?" A: "Yes!"

Q: "What should I be doing?" A: "Write a book!!"

He ruminated on the book calling through more solos until one day he got a blinding glimpse of the obvious. He clarified that he was here, now, "to be a career doorway to the new millennium." He quickly penned a book proposal and the phone started immediately ringing. He received eight calls in seven days relating to the book topic.

If we are sincere in our intention and open to change, we will soon find that the solo experience will become easier and more flowing and we will look forward to being by ourselves. "What we brood over, hatches out!" What this means from a practical standpoint is that we always attract into our lives whatever we think about the most, believe in most strongly, or expect on the deepest levels. Try it daily for a week with an open mind and heart, and then judge whether it is useful.

If we continue using and developing the solo habit, soon the changes in ourselves and in our sense of purpose will become an integral part of our day. It becomes a continuous awareness, a state of "purposeful presence." The solo is one of the most powerful tools we have at our disposal. Our mind and the images within it determine the power of purpose.

THE AGE OF PURPOSE

Whom would you cry out to if you were in an airplane that was suddenly diving toward the ground?

—BRADFORD KEENEY

We are living through the closing chapters of the industrial age, and we are in the opening chapters of the purpose age—a new challenge to reinvent work and the workplace. It is a time of discovery, a time for courageous conversations. In the 21st century, in our shift to a new global economy and new technology-driven world, we need to ask: Is purpose relevant? Is it essential to our lives?

Conversations today about the place and meaning of work abound. We're living in an age when people from many parts of the world are seeking a new perspective on the role of work in their lives. In the 21st century, purpose has the marks of a movement—an inner-directed revolution. It is, I believe, The Age of Purpose. This is an age of inside-out searching that involves discovering our gifts, discovering what moves us, and discovering our callings.

Discovering personal purpose is a cradle-to-grave journey. To explore purpose, we can look to people who walked before us for guidance. Bill Goodwin has frequented the skyways across the country on a regular basis for the past ten years. Yet, like most frequent flyers, he rarely had given much thought to *not* reaching his destination. He assumed the odds of going down in an airplane were very small. If that's true, then imagine what the odds are of walking away from the boarding gate of an aircraft destined to crash. That infinitesimal chance caught up with Bill and spared his life.

Flight 427 was scheduled to depart Chicago's O'Hare Airport at 4:50 P.M. on a hectic Friday afternoon. Bill was on his way to Pittsburgh to attend his first meeting of the executive committee of a college board of trustees. Just before flight time, above the din of a busy O'Hare, Bill heard a page that asked him to check with the nearest gate agent. He was instructed to call his office immediately, where he learned that his first-ever meeting was canceled—the first such cancellation in eleven years!

Shortly before Flight 427 was to begin boarding, Bill turned in his boarding pass and made a quick exit to another concourse where his assistant, Nancy, had booked him on a flight back to his hometown of Atlanta. Soon after arrival, he called his wife Valerie on his car phone on the way home and was greeted by an outburst of tears and raw emotion. "Bill," she sobbed, "you haven't heard; the plane you were supposed to be on to Pittsburgh has crashed short of the airport and no one survived."

Bill was stunned. In that moment on the freeway, he said, "There was only this amazing calm, a sense of peace that settled over me and affirmed that God was holding me in the palm of his hand. . . . I knew that God had taken me off that plane." Arriving home to tears of joy and hugs that didn't want to quit, the television brought the bitter details of Flight 427 into their living room.

Bill reflects, "I know my reprieve is temporary. My life has been extended for now."

Bill believes that God has something more to accomplish through his life. On Monday, after his narrow escape, he got a hint of what that purpose might be. He was besieged by friends, staff, and agents from his insurance agency, all expressing gratitude for his role in their lives. Already the general agent of one of the largest, most successful insurance agencies in the country, Bill realized at that moment that his true purpose, from here on, was to "grow values-driven people." That's the mission of his life and agency. Bill focuses his newly precious time on coaching people to live aligned with their purpose. And he is living true to himself, true to his calling.

As people like Bill Goodwin mature, their purpose becomes deeper, richer, and more caring. Their purpose begins with their genuine desire to connect with the greatest good both within themselves and in their work. Charles Handy, in *The Age of Paradox*, wrote:

> True fulfillment is, I believe, vicarious. We get our deepest
> satisfaction from the fulfillment and growth and happiness of
> others. It takes time, often a lifetime, to realize this. Parents
> know it well, as do teachers, great managers, and all who care
> for the downtrodden and unfortunate.

Caring is at the heart of The Age of Purpose. If we are to have a livable, sustainable world for the 21st century, purpose, the care for others as much as for ourselves, must become our guiding ethic. We each need to discover our calling, to strengthen our capacity for caring.

In our journey toward purpose, our sense of the bigger picture evolves. The more true we are to our purpose, the more likely we are to see the bigger picture. We see the pattern we missed earlier in our lives. We see the interconnectedness of our work and the work of others in the world. We see that the bigger picture includes all people, all cultures, and all religions on the planet.

Knowing who we are, why we are here, and what we're trying to do with our lives enriches our journey. Whether our purpose is to serve God, to raise healthy children, to create a healthier environment, or to play beautiful music, we are empowered by the purpose.

We may not always see the results our work has on others, but we know deep down that there is some contribution, large or small, to the bigger picture. We know that we made a difference, that our life mattered.

Purpose evolves over our lifetime. As it is discovered and rediscovered, it becomes a sense of joy. We are not burdened by it as a sense of duty or moral obligation. We care because it is the natural, healthy way to be.

The power of purpose is the power of caring. It alone is the greatest of all the gifts we have to offer in the 21st century—The Age of Purpose.

A PURPOSE DISCOVERY GROUP GUIDE

STARTING A PURPOSE DISCOVERY GROUP

A creative way to explore your purpose is to start a Purpose Discovery Group. The purpose of the group is to enjoy exploring *The Power of Purpose* and the pleasure of each other's company. The book serves as a catalyst for thoughtful inquiry and dialogue on purpose.

To start a group, ask four other people to join you. Try to enlist people with one or more of the following qualifications: they are interested in exploring the topic of purpose; you feel comfortable talking openly with them; they will agree to meet with you on a regular basis; they will read the book and answer selected questions before each meeting; and they feel comfortable with dialogue.

The Purpose Discovery Group is patterned after a group that Benjamin Franklin established in 1727. His group, called the Junto, met every Friday night in a room over a tavern in Philadelphia. Franklin claimed the club was "the best School of Philosophy, Morals and Politics that then existed in the Province. . . ." Every meeting opened with a set of "queries" (both pious and practical) with a pause between each, when one might fill and sip a glass of wine. The Junto endured 30 years; Franklin even thought of making it international.

FACILITATING A PURPOSE DISCOVERY GROUP

Purpose Discovery Group meetings can be held around breakfast, lunch, after work, or any time that people can commit to two hours of discussion. Some process suggestions include:

- Ask the people you know or see regularly—friends from work, the neighborhood, community group, or family—to join your group.

- Meet twice a month for two months.

- Have at least five participants.

- Meet for a designated length of time (two hours).

- Designate a leader for each meeting to help the flow of discussion.

- Have a specific assignment before each session.

FOLLOWING A FOUR SESSION FLOW

Session One: The Purpose of Purpose

Read: The Introduction and Part I, pp. 1–41

Do: Before the session, answer the questions on:

            p. 2—"If you could live your life over again, you would . . . ?"

p. 11—"Look ahead. How old do you think you'll live to be?"

p. 28—"My calling in life is . . ."

Discuss: Decide on group leaders/expectations.

Group introductions.

Read the quote on p. 10–11 aloud and discuss it.

Discuss the three presession questions (above).

Session Two: Living on Purpose

Read: Part II, pp. 45–73

Do: Before the session, answer the questions on:

p. 48—"Why do I get up on Monday morning?"

p. 61—An Aliveness Questionnaire

Discuss: Read the quote on p. 49 aloud and discuss it.

Discuss the Purpose Spiral on p. 52:

• Which chamber do you see yourself in?

• What is your core question?

Discuss the Aliveness Questionnaire on p. 61:

• Do you feel "the rapture of being alive"?

Session Three: Working On Purpose

Read: Part III, pp. 77–103

Do: Before the session, answer the questions on:

p. 77—"What are your expectations of work?"

"Is work something to be suffered through and endured?" "Or is work synonymous with a calling?"

p. 91—A Working on Purpose Questionnaire

Discuss: Read the quote on p. 78 aloud and discuss it.

Discuss the Working On Purpose Questionnaire on p. 91:

- "Do you feel the 'power of purpose' at work?"

Session Four: A Path to Purpose

Read: Part IV, pp. 107–140

Do: Review the eight "multiple intelligences" on pp. 116–117:

- Rank-order yourself from 1 to 8 based on what you perceive your natural strengths to be (1 is highest, 8 is lowest).

- Think of an example of a talent that would fit in your #1 area.

Review the nine "passion" questions on pp. 120–121:

Discuss: Read aloud the quote on p. 101 and discuss it.

Discuss the eight "multiple intelligences" on pp. 116–117:

- Compare the top three choices of each group member.

Discuss the nine "passion" questions on pp. 120–121:

- Compare responses to the question, "What moves you?"

- Have each member summarize his or her purpose journey (5 minutes).

Celebrate!

FURTHER READING

Armstrong, Thomas. 7 *Kinds of Smart*. Plume. New York: 1993.

Bateson, Mary Catherine. *Composing a Life*. Plume. New York: 1990.

Block, Peter. *Stewardship: Choosing Service over Self-Interest*. Berrett-Koehler. San Francisco: 1993.

Bolles, Richard. *How to Find Your Mission in Life*. Ten Speed Press. Berkeley, CA: 1991.

Bolles, Richard. *What Color is Your Parachute?*. Ten Speed Press. Berkeley, CA: 1997

Bridges, William. *Transitions*. Addison-Wesley. Reading, MA: 1980.

Caple, John. *Finding the Hat That Fits: How to Turn Your Heart's Desire into Your Life's Work*. Dutton. New York: 1993.

Csikszentmihalyi, Mihalyi. *Flow: The Psychology of Optimal Experience*. Harper & Row. New York: 1990.

Edelman, Marion. *The Measure of Our Success*. HarperPerennial. New York: 1993.

Elgin, Duane. *Voluntary Simplicity*. Wm. Morrow & Co. New York: 1981.

Fox, Matthew. *The Re-Invention of Work: A New Vision of Livelihood for Our Time*. HarperCollins. New York: 1995.

Frankl, Viktor. *Man's Search for Meaning*. Pocket Books. New York: 1977.

Frankl, Viktor. *The Unheard Cry for Meaning*. Touchstone. New York: 1978.

Fromm, Eric. *To Have or To Be*. Harper & Row. New York: 1976.

Gardner, Howard. *Frames of Mind: The Theory of Multiple Intelligences*. Basic Books. New York: 1985.

Gardner, Howard. *Leading Minds: An Anatomy of Leadership*. Basic Books. New York: 1995.

Greenleaf, Robert. *Servant Leadership: A Journey into the Nature of Legitimate Power and Greatness*. Paulist Press. New York: 1977.

Hagberg, Janet, and Leider, Richard. *The Inventurers: Excursions in Life and Renewal* (Revised). Addison-Wesley. Reading, MA: 1988.

Hawley, Jack. *Reawakening the Spirit in Work*. Berrett-Koehler. San Francisco: 1993.

Hillman, James. *The Soul's Code: In Search of Character and Calling*. Random House. New York: 1996.

Hudson, Frederic M. *The Adult Years: Mastering the Art of Self-Renewal*. Jossey-Bass. San Francisco: 1991.

Hudson, Frederic M., and McLean, Pamela D. *Life Launch: A Passionate Guide to the Rest of Your Life*. The Hudson Institute Press. Santa Barbara, CA: 1995.

Kabat-Zinn, Jon. *Wherever You Go, There You Are: Mindful Meditations in Everyday Life*. Hyperion. New York: 1994.

Kaye, Beverly. *Up Is Not the Only Way*. 2nd Ed. Davies-Black Publishers. Palo Alto: 1997.

Keeney, Bradford. *Everyday Soul: Awakening the Spirit in Daily Life*. Riverhead. New York: 1996.

Leider, Richard J. *Life Skills*. Pfeiffer and Company. San Diego: 1994.

Leider, Richard J., and Shapiro, David. *Repacking Your Bags: Lighten Your Load for the Rest of Your Life*. Berrett-Koehler. San Francisco: 1995.

Mason, Marilyn. *Seven Mountains: The Inner Climb to Commitment and Caring*. Dutton. New York: 1997.

Murphy, Pat, and Neill, William. *By Nature's Design*. Chronicle. San Francisco: 1993.

Noer, David. *Breaking Free*. Jossey-Bass. New York: 1996.

Robin, Vickie, and Dominquez, Joe. *Your Money or Your Life: Transforming Your Relationship with Money to Achieving Financial Independence*. Viking. New York: 1992.

Stephan, Naomi. *Fulfill Your Soul's Purpose*. Stillpoint. Walpole, NH: 1994.

Storr, Anthony. *Solitude: A Return to Self*. Free Press. New York: 1988.

Williamson. Marianne. *A return to Love*. HarperCollins. New York: 1992.

Whyte, David. *The Heart Aroused: Poetry and the Preservation of the Soul in Corporate America*. Currency/Doubleday. New York: 1994.

Zambucka, Kristin. *Ano Ano: The Seed*. Mana Publishing. Honolulu, HI: 1984.

CONTINUING ON PURPOSE

Reading a book can be very helpful in the pursuit of purpose, and I hope that this book has been useful to you in discovering yours.

In this book, I have shared what I have learned from many teachers and life stories. I invite you to participate in an on-going conversation "on purpose." If anything in this book touched you, troubled you, or inspired you, please write to tell me. I am interested in hearing about sources, resources, and stories of people living and working "on purpose." I'll respond.

You can carry on the process of *The Power of Purpose* with products and programs offered by The Inventure Group of Minneapolis. The Inventure Group, of which I am a founder and partner, is a training design firm devoted to helping individuals, leaders, and organizations ignite the power of purpose.

The Inventure Group offers:

- Speeches and custom meeting presentations;

- Audiotapes and videotapes;

- Workshops for organizations focusing on working, leading, and teaming on purpose;

- The *On Purpose* journal, a quarterly publication designed to support you in living and working on purpose.

If you wish further information about speeches, workshops or materials, please contact:

The Inventure Group
8500 Normandale Lake Blvd., Suite 1750
Minneapolis, MN 55437
(612) 921-8686
Fax (612) 921-8690
E-mail: Invturegrp@aol.com

INDEX

ABOUT THE AUTHOR

Richard Leider is a founding partner of The Inventure Group, a training firm in Minneapolis, Minnesota, devoted to helping individuals, leaders, and teams discover the power of purpose.

He is a nationally respected author, speaker, career coach, and pioneer in the field of Life/Work Planning. Author and co-author of four books—*The Inventurers, Life Skills, Repacking Your Bags,* and *The Leader of the Future*—his work is often featured in newspapers, magazines, and on radio and television, where he is well known as a spokesman on career and lifestyle strategies for the 21st century. His writing has enabled him to reach a broad international audience with inspiring stories and ideas that can often change people's lives.

Richard has a master's degree in counseling psychology from the University of Northern Colorado and is a nationally certified career counselor. He has a bachelor's degree in psychology from Gustavus Adolphus College, which chose him as "Distinguished Alumni in Human Services."

His clients include many leading Fortune 500 companies. He speaks frequently to diverse audiences in the United States and abroad. Richard has been a long-time board member and consultant with Outward Bound, and he designed and led their popular Life/Career Renewal Course.

For the last 15 years, he has led his own yearly Inventure Expedition backpacking safaris in Tanzania, East Africa. Richard believes each of us was born with a natural reason for being—a purpose—and from birth to death, each of us is on a quest to discover that reason. Through his own purpose—helping people discover their purpose and express their calling—he is dedicated to helping people create meaning in their life and work.